Learning To Listen,
Listening to Learn
Noël Janis-Norton

Learning To Listen, Listening to Learn

Noël Janis-Norton

Barrington Stoke

First published in Great Britain by Barrington Stoke Ltd,
Sandeman House, 55 High Street, Edinburgh, EH1 1SR

www.barringtonstoke.co.uk

ISBN 1-84299-228-7

Edited by Julia Rowlandson
Cover design by Helen Ferguson
Typeset by GreenGate Publishing Services, Tonbridge TN9 2RN
Printed in Great Britain by The Cromwell Press

Contents

Acknowledgements

My heartfelt thanks to all the people who have helped make my dream a reality, my friends, colleagues and supporters at The New Learning Centre:

To Robin Shaw, for being the spiritual midwife who made the birth of this book as easy as possible.

To Gillian Edwards, who has been with me through thick and thin, who has enriched this work with her irresistible enthusiasm and who keeps me laughing.

To Miriam Chachamu, for her astute judgment and her commitment to challenging all assumptions.

And to Michael Rose and Gill Dyer, for all their behind the scenes support.

My family:

To my sister Jill Janis, who played a vital role in the development of these ideas, and who teaches these principles at The Family Learning Centre in Tucson, Arizona.

To my children, Jessica, Jordan and Chloé, whose belief in me keeps me going when I forget to believe in myself.

I dedicate this book to the thousands of children, teachers and parents from whom I have learned so much.

Chapter 1
Setting the scene

1. My purpose in writing this book

As I travel around the United Kingdom leading workshops, I talk to thousands of teachers every year, and I hear the same complaints and issues wherever I go. I hear about pupils who:

- are switched off or very distracted
- can't seem to stay on task
- produce sloppy work and don't take pride in their achievements
- have very immature social skills and do not know how to control their aggression
- don't bother to follow routines or obey rules
- argue, interrupt and don't do what they're told
- are disrespectful, rude, noisy and messy
- come to school for the "social life", not in order to learn
- use a diagnosis of a special educational need as an excuse not to try
- are pre-occupied with computer and video games, super-heroes and fantasy worlds.

First in the United States, and then for the past seventeen years at The New Learning Centre in Britain, I have been teaching the "Calmer, Easier, Happier Teaching and Learning" method to teachers, classroom assistants, tutors, mentors, SENCOs, midday staff, education welfare officers and even headteachers.

The types of classroom problems that have improved when these professionals started using new skills have ranged from the relatively mild (e.g. messy handwriting, poor spelling, lack of confidence, a pupil chatting when he should be working) all the way to the severe (e.g. bullying, school refusal, self-harm, substance misuse, violence) and everything in between (e.g. arguing back, swearing, stealing, name-calling). So I know that these skills work, and I invite you to experiment and find out what they can do for you and your pupils.

In this book I will explain what I have learned over the years about how the language that teachers use affects the behaviour, attention, learning, and social skills of our most worrying pupils. I will show what works to enhance skills and positive attitudes and why it works, as well as what does not work and why.

This book is a companion volume to "In Step With Your Class", which discusses how teachers can influence the behaviour and learning of pupils through establishing and maintaining a "positive, firm and consistent" culture in the classroom.

The concepts and strategies of "Calmer, Easier, Happier Teaching and Learning" are discussed in depth in "In Step With Your Class".

These two books are full of strategies that will improve the co-operation, confidence, motivation, willingness to be considerate and self-reliance of *all* your pupils, even the very challenging ones, regardless of their age, gender, family background, social group, tested IQ, diagnosis or inborn temperament. Of course with some pupils, it will take longer to see positive changes than with others.

I was urged to write down these techniques by the teachers who attended my "Calmer, Easier, Happier Teaching and Learning" workshops. These teachers attended the workshops because they were feeling confused, frustrated and sometimes even afraid, when faced with the all-too-familiar litany of problems. After putting into practice the techniques they learned, they saw dramatic improvements. And they got back in touch with the joy of teaching.

So I have attempted to explain in simple and very specific terms the strategies that I, and by now thousands of other teachers, have found to be effective. I learned most of these techniques at the beginning of my teaching career by observing those rare wonderful teachers who had the gift of transforming reluctant, resistant, rude pupils into focused, enthusiastic learners. With the naivety of youth, I thought to myself, "If they can do it, so can I". So I watched and listened carefully, making detailed notes about what these teachers said and didn't say, how they said it, even how they moved and where they stood. I imitated the good examples that I observed, practising non-stop because I was desperate to avoid becoming one of those angry, frustrated teachers who no longer enjoys teaching. Sooner than I could have ever imagined, I too learned how to bring out the best in even the most disruptive, disaffected pupils.

When I finally got around to reading books on classroom management and discipline, I was delighted to discover that the books endorsed and reinforced the concepts and approaches that I had developed through observation and imitation. Therefore in these two books you will find echoes of the many excellent writers on this complex topic:

- Albert Bandura
- James Block
- Lee and Marlene Carter
- John Dewey
- Rudolf Dreikurs
- Erik Erikson
- Adele Faber and Elaine Mazlish
- Howard Gardner
- Haim Ginott
- William Glasser
- Thomas Gordon
- John Holt
- Frederic Jones
- Jacob Kounin
- Jonathan Kozol
- Richard Lavoie
- Mel Levine
- Carl Rogers
- Robert Rosenthal and Lenore Jacobson
- B.F. Skinner

2. What teachers want to achieve in the classroom

At the beginning of each of my "Calmer, Easier, Happier Teaching and Learning" workshops, I ask teachers to tell me what they would need to have happen in their classrooms to ensure that all pupils learn and to preserve their own sanity. The same "needs" keep coming up again and again. These are the "Big Five" habits that enable learning, in its widest and deepest sense, to take place.

The Big Five habits consist of:
1. Acting politely, considerately and positively, which includes
   - making eye-contact
   - listening
   - helping others
   - not laughing at others' mistakes.
2. Following instructions immediately (without arguing, complaining or asking for exceptions).
3. Remembering and following rules and routines, needing very few prompts.
4. Staying on task.
5. Paying attention to all the details of the task (which is a more precise way of saying "doing one's best").

Wouldn't teaching be an easy job if all of our pupils always did the Big Five? I have no magic wand that can guarantee 100% compliance because our pupils are human, not robots or angels. But how does 90% sound? Most teachers say that they would be absolutely delighted to see the Big Five in their classrooms 90% of the time. My experience and observation show me that when teachers make the training of their pupils in these five habits their *priority, day after day*, the academic progress is as impressive as are the improvements in behaviour and social skills.

Sometimes teachers want to add a few more habits to this list, most notably:
- honesty
- creativity
- communication
- enjoyment of learning.

I have not added these to the list of the Big Five habits because in my experience those additional qualities start to blossom automatically once the Big Five are really happening.

Due to the government's inclusion policy, more and more very problematic pupils are ending up in mainstream classrooms, to the utter dismay of teachers who readily admit that their training and experience have not equipped them with the skills needed to reverse the subtle resistance, the outright refusal to co-operate and the relentless rudeness.

Just as there are multiple factors that contribute to pupils being "easy", so there are many causes of problem behaviour. In Chapter 1 of "In Step with Your Class", I listed many causes, but I emphasised that one of those factors, more than any other I have encountered, is responsible for most of the lethargy, time-wasting, disrespect, aggression, non-co-operation, bullying, and poor work. Here is what I wrote. At the risk of boring or irritating readers of both books, I will repeat myself:

> "Many problems with co-operation and motivation are caused by schools not knowing how to meet the needs of pupils who have subtle specific learning difficulties. Pupils who experience difficulties learning gradually become disaffected, switched off, bored and resentful. As time goes by, they attract more and more criticism, and many carve out a niche for themselves. It is as if they say to themselves, "I can never be good, so I will become the best at being bad". Teachers may say of these pupils, "He's looking for trouble" or "He's itching for a fight". And they are right! These pupils are fighting back, and what is at stake is their self-esteem."

All behaviour is caused. Persistent unacceptable behaviour can only be changed by finding out what is causing it and eliminating the causes or at least reducing their impact. When the pupil no longer has such a strong need for the negative behaviour, it becomes much easier to replace it with a positive habit.

In Chapter Two, we will look closely at a particular cluster of characteristics which is present in many different types of specific learning difficulty. These characteristics impede academic learning, social learning and the development of self-control.

Labels and diagnoses do not accurately describe the complex individuality of each pupil. Two pupils with the same diagnosis may be very different from each other, whilst great similarities may exist between pupils with vastly dissimilar diagnoses. So let's not be blinded by all the new "disorders". Instead, let's focus on noticing each individual's *characteristics*, what that pupil can and cannot do well. Only then will we be able to tackle the problem constructively. This is what the renowned U.S. educator, Dr. Mel Levine, terms "management by profile".

Chapter 3 explores how we can use language for several specific purposes:
- to compensate for weak language processing, reasoning and literacy
- to strengthen weak language processing, reasoning and literacy
- to make it easier for pupils to behave appropriately and to enjoy learning
- to improve social skills.

Chapter 4 explains in detail how to use Descriptive Praise:
- to motivate, inspire, and encourage
- to help pupils learn
- to improve behaviour and social skills
- to build self-confidence
- to foster self-reliance
- to teach attention to detail.

Chapter 5 discusses and illustrates the technique of Reflective Listening, which helps pupils:
- to understand and accept their uncomfortable feelings
- to look for and implement constructive solutions
- to move on after a problem or conflict, forgiving themselves and others.

Chapter 6 shows how teachers can maximise the likelihood of pupils following our instructions.

3. The core beliefs that "Calmer, Easier, Happier Teaching and Learning" is based on

Tick any of the statements you agree with:

❑ Do unto others as you would have them do unto you.

❑ Life does not have to be so painful.

❑ Humans are basically good.

❑ Humans (even children! even teenagers!) want to love, want to be appreciated, want to do their best, want to co-operate, want to contribute, want to be competent, confident and friendly.

❑ Children who like themselves like to behave themselves.

❑ Teaching can be fun every day.

❑ Before we can begin to improve any situation, we need to be brave enough to see it as it really is.

❑ What we resist will persist. What we are reluctant or afraid to deal with will continue to be a problem.

❑ We see things, not as they are, but as *we* are. Our experience of life, and how we feel about life, comes from our *interpretation* of events, much more than from what has actually happened.

❑ Children know what they *want*; adults know what children *need*. Adults have more of the experience, maturity and wisdom needed to decide what is good for children than children do. Therefore, the adult needs to be in charge. Being in charge means making carefully thought-out decisions and then following them through.

❑ Everyday life is full of wonder if we stop to pay attention to the details. It is possible to find something to appreciate and learn in every situation, even painful or uncomfortable ones.

On reflection, you can see that many of these beliefs are held by the important and influential schools of thought the world over. Most of us accept at least some of these principles, even if we have not really given them much thought. Even if you do not hold these beliefs now, you probably once did. Maybe you have rejected these beliefs in recent years as too idealistic or too difficult to put into practice.

We *can* live up to our ideals; we *can* recapture the enthusiasm we had when we began teaching. There are techniques, tried and tested, which do make teaching more fun and more effective.

The techniques outlined are not intended to replace the services of health or education professionals. These methods cannot, and are not intended to, diagnose, medically treat, cure or prevent any medical or neurodevelopmental condition.

It should go without saying, but unfortunately it must be said, that each pupil who exhibits problems with learning, attention, behaviour or social skills needs to be thoroughly assessed and treated by a multi-disciplinary team, which might consist of:
- Teacher
- Special educational needs co-ordinator
- General practitioner
- Educational psychologist
- Speech and language therapist
- Occupational and/or physiotherapist
- Neurologist
- Clinical psychologist.

If such assessments became the norm, it would soon be obvious to parents and teachers and to the pupil himself that we cannot compartmentalise the problems. We cannot simply say, "This pupil has a social skills problem" or "He's just a dreamer" or "Of course he's aggressive – look at his home life". Multi-disciplinary assessments reveal that problems with learning, attention, behaviour and social skills tend, overwhelmingly, to show up in the *same pupils*.

My aim is to help you and everyone who works with children and teenagers to be more effective and to enjoy your job more. Please share with us what changes occur when you put these skills into practice so that we may use your experiences to help others. You can fill in the feedback form on our website (you will find details at the back of this book), explaining which techniques you used and for how long, and what the results have been.

Chapter 2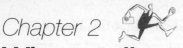
Why pupils misbehave

1. Looking at misbehaviour from a different angle

In a typical classroom, we may see a small handful or so of pupils who could be described as ideal pupils. They do their work, they enjoy learning, they follow the rules, and they get on with their peers. They're not perfect, and they are not always even particularly able. But they are *easy* to teach. Why are some pupils like this? It could be that:

- They do not have much trouble paying attention, so they are usually on task, which leads to success, which leads to self-confidence and to even greater willingness and effort.
- They are relatively easy-going, so they don't mind too much having to do what they are told, even when they don't particularly enjoy it.
- They have the usual childhood impulses (to talk loudly, move around, touch things and change the subject to one that interests them more), but these urges are mild, not strong, so they can resist temptation.
- They find it easy to "behave", so by and large they "do the right thing". They receive lots of approval for it, which motivates them to do even more of the right things. In time they drift into the habit of mostly doing the right things.
- They are self-confident enough to enjoy the challenge of doing their best.
- Their natural curiosity has been encouraged by their parents and their previous teachers, not stifled.
- They trust and respect their teachers because their school experiences have been largely positive.

- They may be fortunate enough to be particularly interested in certain subjects or topics.
- Some are keenly competitive about grades and marks.
- Some have parents who have made them accountable in terms of performance.
- A rare few have the maturity to realise how important learning is for their future.

Most of the pupils we teach will not be this highly motivated or this enthusiastic, of course. But the majority are usually motivated enough to get on with the task at hand, if they are able to. Slowly and steadily they learn and improve.

As we all know, there is yet another sub-section of the class, the pupils who are the exact opposite of easy. These are the children and teenagers who repeatedly make problems for themselves, their teachers, their classmates and, on occasion, for anyone who happens to cross their path. In my experience, most of these unco-operative, unmotivated pupils find learning *at school* difficult, even though they may be bright and may be quite knowledgeable or skilled in non-curriculum matters. These pupils are now considered to have "specific learning difficulties" or to be "atypical learners" because they have an inborn cognitive style (a profile of learning strengths and learning weaknesses) that unfortunately does not "fit" with what is happening in many classrooms. It is these weaknesses, of course, that cause the learning problems and social difficulties, as well as the accompanying feelings of confusion, frustration, shame and anger, and, eventually, the wide range of misbehaviour, both minor and major.

2. Cognitive processing weaknesses

On the most basic level, learning means taking in information through our five senses (sometimes called processing channels), understanding the information, remembering it and being able to do something with it. Pupils without learning difficulties take in, understand, remember and use information relatively well however we present it. In the context of the classroom, this usually means that they know what we are talking about and can talk about it with clarity, and that they understand what they read and can write about it with clarity.

Having a specific learning difficulty (regardless of the diagnosis or label) means that one or more of the five cognitive processing channels is significantly less efficient at registering, understanding, retaining and using information.

In most specific learning difficulties, the weakest processing channel is the auditory channel. This is unfortunate because so much information in the typical classroom is presented orally. The pupil with auditory processing deficits is at a huge disadvantage. He frequently has problems in the areas of:

a) Listening and understanding
   - Has difficulty following verbal instructions because he registers only part of what he hears.
   - Does not even realise that he is not listening carefully and therefore not understanding.
   - Wants to start work before listening to all the instructions.
   - Can follow instructions better after he has been shown how, rather than just told how.
   - Does not connect what he has been taught previously to what he is hearing now.
   - Does not understand the significance of what he hears.
   - Has problems with abstract reasoning; his thinking is concrete and literal.
   - Is very slow to respond; needs time to mull over the question.
   - Seems not to be listening.
   - May watch the teacher's face intently, trying to lip-read.
   - Fidgets inordinately when required to listen for more than a few minutes.
   - Has never enjoyed being read to.

b) Memory
- Forgets what he hears.
- Has not memorised number bonds or multiplication tables when others his age have.
- Has poor comprehension of time and dates (yesterday, tomorrow, next month, seasons, holidays).
- Has difficulty learning rote-memory tasks accurately (e.g. the alphabet, his address, historical dates, poems, prayers, months of the year) so tries to avoid being found out.

c) Speaking
- Makes grammatical or syntactical errors which do not reflect those of his parents, e.g. "more happier, baddest, brang, holded".
- May use small words, such as prepositions, incorrectly.
- May sequence sounds or syllables incorrectly.
- Relies on substitute terms for nouns (whatsit, gizmo, thingy).
- Mispronounces commonly used words.
- Uses incorrect plural endings, e.g. mouses, dices.
- At inappropriate times may hum loudly, talk to himself or make "cartoon noises".
- Has too loud or too soft a speaking voice.
- May have a speech articulation problem, e.g. he may mumble, "swallow" his words or have a lisp.
- Says, "You know what I mean?" repeatedly.

d) Reading
- Has a poor memory for letter names or sounds.
- Has difficulty with sound blending and/or segmentation.
- Expressionless oral reading.
- Has a poor sense of similarity and difference in sounds.
- Has to put so much effort into decoding that he does not have much "brain space" left over for paying attention to the meaning.

As a result of the above difficulties with taking in information through the auditory channel, these pupils are often uncommunicative. They:

- seldom contribute meaningfully to classroom discussions
- respond hesitantly or with one-word answers
- may talk a lot, but express few ideas
- offer responses that do not quite make sense
- may raise their hands enthusiastically to contribute but give answers that are tangential, confused or irrelevant
- repeat themselves or talk too much in a desperate attempt to make themselves understood
- have great difficulty verbalising the reasons for their answers.

In addition to auditory processing problems, many pupils with specific learning difficulties have very immature fine-motor control. This is most apparent in handwriting (although it can also cause problems with dressing, drawing, eating, catching a ball, balance and practical subjects like Science or Information Technology). Often, the handwriting of the "atypical learner" is rushed and illegible. Watching him tackle a writing task, one can sense that he is hurrying to get it over with, paying no attention to spelling, punctuation, sentence construction or even to whether his words make sense. Occasionally, a pupil with fine-motor problems will develop the habit of writing very, very slowly and carefully and neatly. This requires such concentration that there is no room in his head for anything else, so once again we see a pupil who makes "careless" mistakes with his spelling, punctuation, sentence construction, sequencing, etc.

3. Observable classroom behaviour typical of pupils with specific learning difficulties

Teachers often tell me that knowing a pupil's diagnosis is not particularly helpful; what teachers really need are strategies for dealing with the characteristics as these manifest in the classroom.

In the companion volume, "In Step with Your Class", I discussed the ways that specific learning difficulties show themselves in the classroom.

To recap, these are:

Learning

This pupil often has problems with:

- concentration
- organisation
- sequencing
- short-term memory and working memory
- spoken language
- all aspects of literacy.

Behaviour and social skills

This pupil often is:

- off task
- attention-seeking
- egocentric
- absorbed in his own narrow interests
- inflexible
- socially immature
- unrealistic
- the class clown
- stuck in the habit of "learned helplessness"
- afraid of failure and also afraid of success.

I explored why and how lack of academic success leads to problems with behaviour, social skills, respect for authority, and ultimately self-esteem. Chronic and pervasive low self-esteem is the bitter legacy of school difficulties. An adult who found that he was continually failing to do his job properly and was regularly being told off and punished would soon resign and find himself a new job, easier and less stressful, where he could feel more successful. School is the "job" of children and teenagers, but when things go badly wrong with learning or behaviour or peer relationships, our pupils cannot change jobs.

Anger, hopelessness, desperation, anxiety, passive or active resistance – these are all aspects of low self-esteem, and they tend to manifest in the classroom in predictable ways. The three main behavioural categories are:

Avoidance tactics

These may include:

- doing the bare minimum
- not even trying to pay attention
- dawdling, seeming not to hear instructions
- writing answers to the easy questions but leaving the more difficult items blank
- not seeming to remember often-stated expectations (e.g. neatness counts; show all the steps in a mathematics problem; indent the beginning of paragraphs; use complete sentences)
- managing to get 'C' grades, but it is obvious that he does not really understand and remember the information or skill
- coming up with weak excuses to avoid doing his work and seeming to believe these are valid reasons
- copying from the textbook instead of writing the answers in his own words
- doing his homework but forgetting to bring it in to school.

Negative attention seeking

This might be:

- boasting
- calling out
- bothering other pupils, either overtly or subtly
- acting the clown
- saying "I can't"
- asking unnecessary questions that he should be able to figure out the answers to, such as:
  - Is this going to be on the exam?
  - What's today's date?
  - Why do we have to do this?
  - How do you spell…?
  - What are we doing next?
- getting out of his seat
- being late unnecessarily
- interrupting, arguing, complaining, ridiculing
- over-reacting.

Defiance and refusal

This might involve:

- not doing homework or classwork
- giving far-fetched excuses without seeming even to care whether you believe him
- swearing
- truanting
- walking out of the classroom without permission
- threats, swearing, racist or sexist remarks
- intimidating body language
- damaging property and hurting people
- violence.

Regardless of how many of these disturbing classroom characteristics you are struggling to cope with at present, it is possible to significantly improve your pupils' motivation and co-operation in the very near future. Through the "Calmer, Easier, Happier Teaching and Learning" programme, I have seen that, with training in certain techniques, teachers *can* achieve their goals for their pupils, and teachers can enjoy teaching more. Others have succeeded and so can you. Just by starting to read this book you are taking the next steps on an exciting, rewarding path.

4. Typical strengths of "atypical" learners

As an antidote to the detailed list of difficulties I have just described, let's remember that even a very problematic pupil is not just one big bundle of problems. Each pupil has strengths as well as weaknesses. Teachers consistently find that many pupils who exhibit problems with learning, attention, behaviour and social skills also share the following strengths. This pupil:

- May seem very bright outside of school; he is able to do many more things than the teacher would expect.
- Is often creative and inventive, given to lateral thinking.
- Constantly monitors the environment; he has excellent attention to detail for novel aspects of the environment and for

things that interest him; he reacts quickly (except to orally presented instructions).

- Is capable of extreme focus (in self-chosen activities).
- Is able to change strategies quickly (usually only in self-chosen activities).
- Has a high energy level (which can, of course be a problem, for example when the restless pupil annoys his classmates by tapping, drumming, scratching, picking at his scabs, leg-swinging, etc.).
- Is usually a strong picture thinker, able to visualise accurately and vividly.
- Loves excitement and has a keen sense of adventure (for self-chosen activities).
- May face danger willingly (the downside may be recklessness or showing off).
- Can be giving, affectionate and caring.
- Often has a good long-term memory (although what goes into it is often unrelated to school matters).
- Is often talented, usually in art, sports or music (but rarely has the patience to practise regularly or the maturity to admit and correct his mistakes, so he often does not progress from talented to skilled).
- Often has a strong sense of humour and fun (which he may not know how to save for the appropriate times and places).

As can be seen, the same characteristic can be a useful resource in one situation and a liability in another situation. For example, a lateral thinker with a keen sense of fun can become addicted to having the last word, readily coming up with an alternative and more humorous interpretation for everything you say, and then sitting back and soaking up the laughter of his classmates.

Just as not every pupil has every characteristic of specific learning difficulties, not all pupils with problems will have all these strengths.

However, with their very real strengths, it certainly should be possible for schools to help these pupils to relax, drop the chips from their shoulders and start to feel confident. However, this will not happen as long as they are being given work to do that is too difficult for their weakest processing abilities.

Chapter 3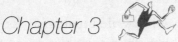

Improving pupils' behaviour, learning, and social skills through the conscious use of language

1. Why do teachers need to consciously modify the language of teaching?

When we start to think about how we speak, we realise that it is not enough just to say that we use language to teach. Within that broad canvas, we are attempting to do many subtly different tasks. For example, on any given day we will need to:

- introduce
- describe
- define
- explain
- sequence events, narrate
- show relationships and connections
- organise, categorise
- tell pupils what to do
- tell pupils how to do something
- emphasise
- correct.

And then there are our less tangible aims, and for all of these, language is our medium. We aim to:

- guide
- motivate
- inspire
- reassure

- encourage
- boost self-esteem.

For the majority of pupils, our usual way of talking is probably adequate to accomplish all of the above goals. Sadly, in mainstream classrooms pupils with special educational needs and behavioural problems are often left far behind, confused, frustrated and not even able to explain coherently that they are not really grasping the essentials of what we are trying to teach.

Simple but extensive modifications to the language of teaching will help pupils in several ways:

- The modifications will ease the processing load for pupils with auditory channel weaknesses and concentration problems. (This technique is often called compensation or by-passing.)
- Even more importantly, the changes that I propose will teach and train these pupils to use their auditory processing channel more effectively.
- In addition, the language modifications I outline will make it easier for *all* pupils to pay attention, understand, remember, use their knowledge and skills and enjoy learning.

The results of these language modifications often are:

- more enjoyment of learning
- improvements in behaviour, attitudes and social skills
- a greater eagerness for challenge
- more time spent on task
- more solid academic achievement
- a calmer, kinder class.

The way we speak is largely a matter of habit. To reach and teach pupils with cognitive processing deficits we need to make a conscious, consistent effort to "upgrade" our habitual ways of speaking.

2. Receptive language difficulties: How can we consciously use language to compensate for and improve weak receptive language processing?

2a. The teacher's voice

- Speak more slowly than usual, with longer pauses between sentences and also between phrases within each sentence.
- Speak clearly; "mouth" your words. This will help pupils with auditory discrimination problems to differentiate more easily between words that sound similar.
- Keep your voice at a moderate level because this pupil often has as much difficulty understanding shouting as he does understanding a low voice.
- Without shouting, project your voice so that it carries easily to every corner of the classroom, even when you are having a one-to-one conversation (unless it is a particularly private conversation, of course). This has the added bonus of helping your pupils to see you as the one in charge.
- Making sure that you sound the last consonant in every word helps clarity.
- Use the tone of voice you would use with a stranger: polite and calm, not impatient, irritated, abrupt or cold.
- Make your voice enthusiastic. If the teacher doesn't seem involved and interested, how can we ever hope that the pupils will be?
- During the lesson, vary the tone, pace and register of your voice to keep pupils interested.

2b. Reducing distractibility and impulsivity by using language to highlight the most important points of the lesson

- Make sure that all pupils have finished the last activity before you start talking about the next activity. The very pupils who are slowest to complete tasks or tidy up are often the ones who most need to be paying full attention to your next instructions in order to "hear", understand and comply.

- Use an attention-getting device before asking questions or giving an instruction. For an individual pupil, pointing to him or moving closer to him or in front of him is friendlier and calmer than saying his name, which can sound accusatory. For the class as a whole, your attention-getting device can be waiting. Both for individuals and for groups, using the opportunity to Descriptively Praise while you wait is often the most effective way to get their attention. See Chapter 4 for ideas on how you can use Descriptive Praise to get and keep your pupils' attention.
- Make sure to get and give eye contact before asking questions or giving instructions.
- Have the pupils face you squarely before you speak. Be aware that some pupils, especially those on the autistic spectrum, may experience mild or even acute sensory overload when required to look and listen at the same time. This can lead to confusion, irritability, switching off or even severe misbehaviour (sometimes in the hope of being sent out of the classroom). Because making eye contact is such an essential social skill, I do not recommend exempting these pupils from the requirement to look at the person who is speaking. We can teach such pupils to become more accustomed to, and more comfortable with, making eye contact. Because this is truly difficult for these pupils, the teaching and training needs to be accomplished in a number of small gradual stages:
    1. Prepare for success by acknowledging, if it is true, that you know that the pupil is trying to listen even though he is not looking towards the speaker.
    2. Explain what society's expectations are and why society puts such a high value on eye contact.
    3. Do not move onto the next stage until this pupil can easily explain back to you, without reminders or prompting, what those expectations are and why.
    4. Teach this pupil two separate strategies:
        a) Focus on a far-off speaker's neck or shoulders or look slightly to the side of the speaker.

b) When the pupil is a conversational distance away from the speaker, he can be taught to focus on the speaker's nose. By using these steps even pupils with a neurologically based aversion to eye contact can be helped to look the speaker in the eye, at first for a fleeting moment, then over time for additional seconds.

- When speaking to a very distractible pupil, place yourself so that there is very little visual stimuli behind you, e.g. a blank whiteboard.

- To block out some of the competing visual stimuli before you speak to this pupil one-to-one, place your hands slightly in front of and on either side of his face, without touching.

- Give several summary sentences as an introduction before beginning a discussion or a set of instructions so that pupils will know what to pay attention to and what to visualise.

- Carefully relate new activities or information to previously learned knowledge so that pupils can build on what they already understand. Do this by asking questions, rather than by telling. The more that pupils are required to think, to remember and to make connections, the better they will understand and the more accurately they will remember.

- Write out instructions or the steps of a procedure on a piece of card for a distractible pupil to keep on his desk and refer to. If many pupils in a class need this support, make a poster that stays on the wall only while it is relevant. Take the poster down when it is not being used so that pupils see it with fresh eyes each time you show it.

- Give verbal instructions as you demonstrate what to do and how do it.

- Give a running commentary as one pupil demonstrates for the class what to do and how to do it.

- Verbal "mannerism cues" can be used to indicate that something important is coming up. For example, you might:
  - repeat the words or phrases for emphasis
  - spell out important words

- write a list on the board
- read a list, allowing time to take notes
- speak even more slowly
- speak even more loudly
- emphasise certain words
- use a different tone of voice
- ask rhetorical questions (not meant to be answered).

2c. Vocabulary and sentence construction

- Speak in shorter sentences.
- Speak in simpler sentences.
- Speak in complete sentences. This may seem very obvious advice, but many people, including many teachers, regularly start sentences that they do not finish. Training yourself to always finish every sentence you start may feel awkward at first but will result in smooth, easy, articulate communication.
- Give very short explanations.
- Use concrete and vivid vocabulary to tap into the relative visualisation strengths of pupils with weak auditory processing.
- Use repetitive speech patterns so that your language becomes predictable.
- In speaking, replace pronouns with nouns. This makes the topic or point easier for the pupil to visualise (as otherwise he may soon forget what a particular pronoun refers to). This technique will greatly aid comprehension. It will also make your speech sound more measured and more "important", which helps you to be perceived as the person in charge.
- Repeat key words, phrases and sentences many times. Ask questions that require the pupils to also repeat them. Inject variety into the repetition to keep pupils on their toes.
- Before teaching any new information or concept, pre-teach any specialised or unfamiliar vocabulary; otherwise, pupils with receptive language difficulties are faced with two difficult tasks: understanding the content of the lesson and understanding the vocabulary used.

- To teach new vocabulary use vocabulary that the pupils are familiar with and already understand.
- To reinforce new vocabulary, have all pupils do a quick "pair-share", during which they each say in their own words what the new words mean.
- Keep in mind the literalness of many pupils with learning, attention and behaviour problems. You will need to define many unfamiliar words and phrases that you might think they should already be familiar with. For example:
  - idioms: e.g.
    - It's raining cats and dogs.
    - He flew out the door.
    - I take my hat off to you.
  - metaphors: e.g.
    - all hands on deck
    - steer the conversation
    - storm in a tea cup.
  - similes: e.g.
    - like water off a duck's back
    - as slippery as an eel
    - sticks out like sore thumb.
  - sayings, e.g.
    - Don't put all your eggs in one basket.
    - Rome wasn't built in a day.
    - He who hesitates is lost.
  - abstract ideas: e.g.
    - democracy
    - growth
    - respect
    - happiness.
- You can teach new vocabulary by giving a synonym and then immediately asking for the meaning. You can say:
  "Create means make. Another word for 'create' is…?
  Another word for 'make' is…?"

- Make a game of having pupils tell you: "The most important or key word (or phrase) in this sentence is _____."
- Use formal language (also known as "school talk" or "talking like a book") alongside more informal vocabulary and sentence construction so that pupils learn, in a sense, to be "bi-lingual". Make explicit the differences amongst types of language and the accepted occasions for the use of each. We can teach pupils that there are many different ways of conveying the same meaning. We can help them to realise that all teachers express themselves slightly differently, and that this will also be true of their employers one day.

2d. Answering pupils' questions

There are three distinct kinds of question we need to deal with:

A. Legitimate questions that pupils ask.

B. Legitimate questions that pupils need to ask but are too confused or anxious to even voice.

C. Unnecessary questions.

A. It often happens that a concept or procedure which is simple and obvious to the teacher and to the majority of pupils is not getting through to the pupil who has a processing weakness. To make matters worse, when this pupil experiences the discomfort of confusion and frustration his mind may shut down. When pupils say the following, often they are, without even realising it, abdicating responsibility for thinking. They are expecting the teacher to do all the work.

- I don't understand.
- I don't get it.
- This doesn't make sense.
- What do I do?
- It's too hard.
- This is boring.
- This is stupid.

We have two jobs here. One is to teach pupils how to ask for help when they are having difficulties with a task. We need to show that complaining, insulting, giving up or acting helpless are not effective ways of getting us to help them. Our other job is to help them develop the habits of clear thinking.

Here is what I suggest:

1. Recognise that the pupil probably feels anxious or embarrassed, even though he may be hiding his feelings under a mask of indifference or defiance. Take the time, and make the effort, to understand how he is feeling. (Reflective Listening is useful for this, see Chapter 5.)

2. Do not say or imply that you expected the pupil to already know that skill (or fact, strategy, etc.), even if the other pupils mastered it years ago. It is not the pupil's fault that he has poor thinking skills or gives up easily. Instead, say something like, "Oh, I see I need to teach you this". This will help the pupil to feel that you are on his side; he will realise that you do not expect him to know what he has not yet learned.

3. Do not expect the pupil to be able to tell you what it is that he does not understand, or at what point he became confused. When a pupil does not understand what we say, it is our job to figure out at what point he fell by the wayside.

4. If you are feeling rushed or stressed, you may resort to simply repeating yourself. This is unlikely to help; if the pupil did not understand the original explanation or instruction, he is unlikely to understand a simple repetition. (If, on the other hand, you think he was not paying attention, see B on page 30.) Rather than repeating, start again at the beginning or at least at a much lower level or at an earlier stage in a sequence. But instead of you doing the talking, ask questions that require the pupil to explain it to you, in his own words. Keep asking him what he *does* know and understand. Feedback from the pupil is the most accurate gauge of his understanding and memory. You will soon spot where and how the confusion arose.

If you are worried that this process would take too much time because you would have to start so far back, this is a very strong sign that the pupil is being given the wrong work. All pupils deserve to be given work that they have a very high probability of doing well with very, very little confusion.

5. When you reach the area of confusion, have your pupil practise making a polite, specific request:
   - Why does that happen?
   - Please say it again.
   - Please say that more slowly.
   - Could you say that in a different way, please?
   - Please show me the next step.
   - What does that word mean?

   Learning how to make polite, specific requests is one of the most useful skills for later life, both for employment and for relationships.

6. At this point, you can re-teach, but not before! When we try to explain before we know where the confusion is coming from, we waste their time and ours and often end up creating even more confusion and frustration.

7. Do not say, "Do you understand?" Instead, at each step take the time to have the pupil paraphrase what you said. That way you can make sure he has understood. He needs to say it in his own words because exact repetition may be parroting without comprehension.

8. Use a question from one pupil as an opportunity for the whole table or whole class to receive clarification or reinforcement. Other pupils may also be confused about the same point but are not feeling brave enough, concerned enough or interested enough to put their hands up and ask. When the teacher explains a point to one pupil, other pupils nearby will often eavesdrop. They may actually absorb more this way than if they were addressed directly because there is often less anxiety, and

therefore less resistance, when the pupil is not being addressed directly. So remember that you have a wider audience, and phrase your statements and questions so that they can be understood by all the pupils.

9. Do not let impatience or frustration build up, either for you or for the pupil. Taking small steps, and arranging your lessons so that the pupil experiences many small successes, will go a long way toward ensuring an enthusiastic, or at least a willing, pupil.

10. If necessary, take a break from that particular point to give yourself time to think about a new way of teaching it, if possible in a more concrete way.

B. Often a pupil with processing difficulties will seem to be just sitting there, avoiding getting started, when in fact his brain is fully occupied with translating the words he has just heard into mental pictures that he can access more easily. As long as this pupil is not doing anything disruptive or against the rules, be prepared to wait up to 15 seconds. (This is much longer than you would think!)

Then, if you can see that the pupil is still having difficulty understanding the work or staying motivated, you can make the task more do-able, more meaningful and more enjoyable. One way is to combine Reflective Listening with attempts to clarify what the problem is:

- "I might be talking too fast for you. Maybe you would like me to say it again more slowly."
- "I just used some new words; that might have confused you. Would you like someone to explain what _____ means?"
- "It might be hard for you to understand just by listening. Maybe it would help if someone shows you as well."

Then have the pupil practise asking politely and specifically for what he needs. Chapter 5 gives more examples of Reflective Listening.

C. However, as teachers know only too well, many questions do not reflect true confusion. A question can be an avoidance strategy, an attention-seeking device, a delaying tactic or a wind-up. These questions are often repetitive, tangential or completely irrelevant. Many questions (and complaints) arise from:

- not having listened carefully
- not remembering something
- an anxious need for constant approval (as compared to using "common sense" and getting on with the task)
- trying to bargain or hoping for an exception.

When a pupil asks one of these unnecessary questions, we are presented with a golden opportunity to help him learn to think, and in the process to become more self-reliant and more self-confident. So we need to resist the temptation to save precious time by giving him a quick answer or simply repeating ourselves. His brain needs to *work* for the answer. By having to grapple with the question, by making the effort to think about it, trying to remember or taking a guess or looking it up, he will be learning how to learn. As a result, he will understand more and remember more. And, just as important for the teacher's sanity, he will soon be asking fewer and fewer silly questions.

Once again, instead of answering the unnecessary question, ask questions of your own. Asking the class to take a guess is very effective because it immediately puts the focus on a sensible response. At this point, the very pupil who drives you mad with his endless silly questions will probably surprise you by raising his hand and hazarding a sensible guess. That is because suddenly the focus has shifted, and being willing to guess and think sensibly is being rewarded with positive attention. Even very resistant pupils will eventually gravitate towards your positive attention once they see that it is within their power to attain it. As long as the pupil is really trying to guess, find something to Descriptively Praise, even in the most tangential or incorrect response. You can always Descriptively Praise the pupil's courage in guessing.

2e. Verbal cues

- **Emphasis cues** are those which the teacher uses to focus attention on important information, e.g.:
  - You need to know...
  - You need to note...
  - You need to understand...
  - You need to remember...
  - You need to underline...
  - You need to think about...
  - This is important...
  - This is key...
  - This is basic...
  - Listen carefully...
  - Let me emphasise...
  - Let me repeat...
  - Let me explain...
  - Let me make clear...
  - Why is it that...?
  - Now why do you think this is so?

- **Organisational cues** are those which are given to help the pupils understand the order, sequence or relationship of the information being given, e.g.:
  - The topic is...
  - Today we shall discuss...
  - To introduce...
  - First of all...
  - Second, third, etc. ...
  - Then...
  - Next...
  - As a result...
  - Because of this...
  - The main headings we will discuss are...
  - Several important points are...
  - In the following order...
  - In conclusion...

      – To summarise…
      – To review…
      – To recap…
      – To go over…

3. Expressive language difficulties: How can we consciously use language to compensate for and improve weak expressive language processing?

Here is a question I hear a lot, with many variations:

> "I have a few pupils who often ruin the lesson for all the others by impulsively answering without thinking, often calling out or interrupting. One of them is desperate to show that he knows everything, one is an attention-seeker, and one does not even seem to care if he gets it right or wrong, as long as he answers first, before anyone else. Telling them off doesn't do any good, although it makes me feel a bit better for a moment. Are you saying these pupils really can change? I'd love to believe it, but I have to admit I'm sceptical because over the years I've tried everything."

My reply:

> Yes, I *am* saying that when we use language consciously and constructively we can significantly improve the receptive and expressive language skills, as well as the attention span, patience and self-control, of pupils with problems.

> However, the teaching and training of accurate and thorough oral responses needs ongoing teacher input. Tackling expressive language skills will test your patience and consistency, but it is, of course, worth it because everything starts improving when language improves: comprehension, motivation, social skills and self-confidence.

In recent years a very positive movement has surfaced in some schools, called the "no hands classroom". It was born from the recognition that when a teacher asks questions of the whole class, it is the same 25% or so who attempt to answer most of the questions. A similar percentage almost never raise their hands to contribute, due to lack of confidence, motivation, fluency or grasp of the material. In the no-hands classroom every single pupil is not just encouraged, but taught and trained and required, to speak up, participate and contribute.

Teachers often ask me what to do about the unsatisfactory nature of pupils' responses to questions. For example, when you ask a question of a pupil with processing deficits, there are a number of typical problematic responses:

- He may remain silent, either making eye contact or looking somewhere else. The reason for his silence might be that:
  - he did not hear the question because he was daydreaming or pre-occupied with a worry or "messing about"
  - he heard you, but did not quite understand the question and does not know how to ask for clarification
  - he understood the question but is not sure of the answer and wants to avoid the embarrassment of a public mistake
  - he knows the answer but is aware that he does not express himself clearly, so is hoping to avoid the teacher becoming impatient or other pupils laughing at him
  - he suffers from extreme shyness, nowadays termed "social anxiety" or "exposure anxiety", embarrassment so crippling that it can result in "selective mutism", in which the person eventually stops talking at all in certain places or situations.
- He may say "I don't know" even when he does know the answer, possibly because:
  - he wants to avoid public exposure
  - he cannot trust that his words will "come out right"
  - he does not want other pupils to think of him as a "nerd, boffin, brainbox or teacher's pet"
  - to an angry resistant pupil, co-operation seems like giving in.

- He may say "I don't know" very quickly, before even thinking about whether he knows the answer or not because:
  - he does not want to risk disapproval or being laughed at
  - he has experienced that his answers are usually wrong.
- He may answer incorrectly because:
  - he impulsively blurts out the first thing that comes into his head, without pausing to think about whether it is correct
  - he does not understand the question
  - he enjoys winding up the teacher even though he did know the correct answer.
- He may answer correctly but incompletely.
- His answer may be a confused and confusing combination of correct, incorrect and irrelevant information.

With all these possible reasons for not answering correctly, it is understandable that teachers become confused, as well as frustrated, irritated and sometimes even despairing. Luckily, there are numerous effective strategies available for the teacher who is determined to engage *all* the pupils. We need to teach all of our pupils how to express themselves clearly and confidently, and we need to ease them into the *habit* of contributing their ideas. All the strategies take time, and they require us to re-think our priorities. The word "priority" originally meant "first" (although it is used nowadays to mean "most important"). I am saying that *first* we need to help our pupils to think clearly and speak clearly, if they are ever to have a chance of mastering the National Curriculum or anything else we want them to learn.

We need to give our pupils focused language practice and immediate, clear, useful feedback so that they learn to express themselves orally, long before we can expect them to be able to do it in their writing. For example, they need to practise:

- introducing
- defining
- describing
- explaining
- narrating
- summarising.

Here are some successful strategies used by teachers:

- Ask short questions.

- Ask lots of questions, especially those which require pupils to explain or predict, rather than simply to recall.

- Elicit several short answers from the same pupil or from different pupils. Give the pupils practice at putting all the information together to construct longer, more complex sentences and, eventually, verbal "paragraphs". For example:

Teacher: Who fought at the battle of Hastings?

Pupil 1: William the Conqueror and Harold.

Teacher: Yes. When did the Battle of Hastings take place?

Pupil 2: 1066.

Teacher: That's right. Now tell me who and when in the same sentence.

Pupil 3: The Battle of Hastings was in 1066 and William the Conqueror and Harold fought each other.

Teacher: You did exactly what I asked. You put several bits of information together in one sentence. Now we'll add a third piece of information. Tell me who and when, the way you just did, and now also tell me why they fought each other.

Pupil 4: In 1066 Harold and William fought the Battle of Hastings because they both wanted to be king.

Teacher: Now that is a mature sentence. It gives the listener lots of information.

- You can boost the confidence of a habitually disengaged, anxious or easily confused pupil by letting him know, before the lesson begins, which questions you will ask him. This will greatly reduce his anxiety and risk of being overwhelmed.

- Let the pupil know (see Chapter 5 on Reflective Listening) that it is natural to be anxious about making mistakes. This is a more effective way to help pupils relax than to lecture about "Everyone makes mistakes. There's no need to be nervous. If you never made mistakes, you would never learn." etc. etc.

- Give pupils written questions (either on the board or on paper) to think about before they have to answer. Require them to mentally rehearse their response in a full sentence before you call on them to answer. In pairs they can practise saying their answers, helping each other to improve before they are expected to speak in front of the group.

- Require full sentences with all relevant information to help pupils visualise connections.

- Require your pupils to speak using more nouns and fewer pronouns in order to help them to visualise more effectively and to teach them to convey full information.

- To practise correct or mature sentence construction and vocabulary, have the pupil repeat sentences with you simultaneously or consecutively.

- Have frequent (both structured and unstructured) paired work and small-group work so that pupils with weak language skills can:
    - hear at close quarters and be influenced by the language of their non-impaired peers
    - speak up with less embarrassment than if they were in front of the whole class.

- To help pupils develop the habit of explaining what they mean, use questions, especially of the type I call "clarification by contrast". For example, you could say, "Was the old shirt grey because it had not been washed for a long time, or was it grey because that was the colour the shirt had always been?".

- Pupils with expressive language difficulties often come to rely on a very narrow vocabulary. If we allow them to continue to express themselves in this limited way, we cannot be surprised if their writing and their thinking also remain limited. One way of expanding vocabulary usage is to make several (removable) posters with the pupils. These might be lists:
    - other words for "nice, fun, good, great, wonderful, terrific"
    - other words for "boring, bad, evil, horrible, terrible, awful"
    - adjectives to use when describing
    - verbs and adverbs to use when narrating
    - interesting link words, especially to replace "then".

- After every few sentences that you say, require pupils to do one of the following:
    - restate in their own words
    - summarise
    - give a synonym for a key word
    - answer a "Why" question.

- When faced with a shy but able pupil, do not rationalise that as long as he does the work and performs well on written exams there is no real need for training fluent oral responses. Shyness can develop into a debilitating problem. Unless effectively tackled, it can lead to depression and to unnecessary under-achievement in later life and to great difficulties with relationships. You need not worry that training an anxious pupil to speak up in class will make him even more anxious and therefore damage him emotionally. Quite the opposite: quickly his self-confidence will blossom as he sees that he can do what all the others are expected, as a matter of course, to do.

- A very effective way to start training a passive pupil, whether shy, unconfident or resistant, to respond to a teacher's questions is by using what I call "trailing statements". Don't ask a pupil, for example, "When was the Battle of Hastings?" if you think he will remain silent or say, "I don't know". Instead you can say, "The Battle of Hastings took place in…" and let your voice trail off as you look at the pupil, without saying his name or pointing to him. If he does not respond by finishing your sentence within a few seconds, you can either finish the sentence yourself or ask another pupil to answer. Because you did not direct a question to the passive pupil, you did not put him on the spot. He has not failed; his passivity has not been reinforced. In a minute or so, come back to him with the *same* trailing statement. After hearing you or another pupil finish the same sentence in the same way two or three times, the shy, unconfident or resistant pupil will eventually feel safe enough to risk finishing the sentence. He is now sure he knows the answer and that no one will laugh, so he will be able to be brave. If you do this in every lesson, within weeks you will be able to ask a direct question of this pupil and receive a sensible response.

Similarly, when a pupil answers incorrectly, tangentially or incompletely, make sure that within a few minutes you return to him with the very same question, and have him respond correctly. Do not assume that he will learn from simply hearing someone else give the correct answer. He needs to say it himself. This way he will learn more about the subject matter being discussed, and he will also learn about the rewards of perseverance. He will be learning how to learn.

- It will sometimes happen that while you are training one pupil to answer you by using a trailing statement or requiring a guess, another pupil will blurt out the answer. Do an Action Replay immediately, so that the blurter practises self-control. An Action Replay consists of "redoing" the incident, but this time the pupil is helped to do it right. For example, you could say,

  > "We'll do that again. I'll ask Thomas the answer. And while I'm waiting for Thomas to answer, what will you do, Sam, instead of calling out?"

  Once Sam can give you a sensible reply, you all do the Action Replay. It is truly experiential learning, and very effective at changing habits. Then continue with the training and make sure that the first pupil paraphrases the answer in his own words, rather than parroting what the blurter said. That way he is learning that he can participate successfully.

- Learn to wait (even 15 seconds!) for delayed responses due to slow processing, instead of assuming that the pupil does not know the answer. Show, by your smile and by your relaxed, attentive stance that it is all right to take time to think before answering. If another pupil giggles, groans or mutters, stop everything and do an Action Replay.

- Always follow up a response of "I don't know" by requiring the pupil to guess. Sometimes telling a pupil to "Take a guess" leads to a deliberately silly answer. Instead of responding with "Don't be ridiculous" or "You're not even trying", I suggest that you say something like, "I realise I should have told you to take a *sensible* guess". This shows that you are not letting yourself get wound up. Then carry on with requiring him to guess.

- Sometimes you will see that a pupil is guessing wildly, rather than trying to remember or trying to figure out the answer. Say that you can see he is guessing. Let him know that this means there is probably something about the question that he does not understand. Then backtrack until you get to the point where his understanding is so solid that he will not feel the need to pluck an answer from the air.

- As long as the pupil is really trying, find something to Descriptively Praise, even when a pupil's answer is incorrect, incomplete or too concrete. Reinforce whatever was correct in the answer by paraphrasing it. Ask other pupils to add more information, and keep paraphrasing the correct bits. Always remember to go back to the first pupil to make sure that, eventually, he answers the question correctly and completely.

- Whenever a pupil makes a "careless" or "foolish" mistake (usually impulsive) about something you know he knows, it is helpful to give what I call a "diagnostic response". This shows him why he made the error, rather than simply correcting him or asking him to try again. The diagnostic response helps him to clear up the misunderstanding that caused the error. For example, if you ask "What is 3 x 9?" and the pupil answers "12", you can say, "No. Maybe you thought I said 'plus' because 3 + 9 does equal 12. But I didn't say 'plus'. What operation did I say?" If he does not know, he needs to take a sensible guess.

4. Social skills problems: How can we consciously use language to compensate for and improve immature social skills (both with peers and with those in authority)?

- Always say "Please" and "Thank you" to set a good example.

- Always wait for the "please" before you hand a pupil anything or reply to a question or a request.

- Any time a pupil does not say "Thank you", do an Action Replay, and then Descriptively Praise.

- To set a good example and boost self-esteem we need to think before we speak. Everything we say to a pupil has an effect. However, we often speak before we have thought through what we want to achieve by our communication, what effect we want our words to have. So let us not waste "the teachable moment" (the reachable moment!) by speaking impulsively. How many times have we all caught ourselves, too late, just after we have said something that we fervently wish we had not said? Unless we monitor ourselves rigorously, much of what we say will be useless repetition, which serves only to irritate the pupils and to undermine their respect for us.

- Remember the old adage about what to do when you feel yourself getting angry: "Count to ten before you speak". This is still good advice for most classroom situations, when you find yourself becoming frustrated or impatient. Counting to ten gives us the time to evaluate the situation and to see what strategy is called for, rather than falling into the old trap of repeating, reminding, nagging, justifying, cajoling, explaining, threatening, etc.

- Speak as politely to your pupils as you would to a stranger. We need to be positive role models, if we expect our pupils to learn to be co-operative, civil and considerate. We can speak politely and pleasantly if we make it a habit to pause before we speak. That will give us the time to remember our goals and our strategies.

- Do not complain, either in words, body language, facial expressions, or tone of voice. In particular, we need to demonstrate cheerfulness when we are doing anything which we believe that we SHOULD do, but do not FEEL like doing, such as playground duty in the drizzling rain or lunchtime duty in a noisy, chaotic lunchroom.

- Use lots of role-plays, rehearsals and Actions Replays to prepare for success. Have pupils practise more mature social skills, rather than reacting *after* the event by telling them what they did wrong, what they should have done or what they should do next time.

5. Body language

5a. What are the components of body language?
- Eye-contact
- Facial expressions
- Gestures
- Posture
- Movement
- Proximity.

5b. Why is body language so important?

Using non-verbal communication consciously and constructively helps us to:
- convey that we are in charge
- make our teaching points more effectively
- keep our pupils interested
- show that we care about our pupils.

5c. How can we consciously use our body language as a tool to help us achieve our goals for our pupils?

Stand up straight, with hands relaxed at your sides. This conveys confidence and authority.

Keep on your feet as much as possible. From a standing position you will have a better vantage-point for noticing details that need to be praised or corrected. You will also project a bigger "presence".

Keep moving around the classroom. This will keep your energy level up. It also establishes you as the focal point of interest as well as the person who is clearly in charge. When you are on the move, the pupils have to pay attention to you because your actions are not quite predictable.

Keep switching your gaze from pupil to pupil to pupil so that it is clear to all that you are always watching everything that is going on in the classroom. This technique will prevent much off-task behaviour and will nip many problems in the bud. A drop in the teacher's awareness can be a signal to pupils that they can now try to get away with inappropriate behaviour or poor performance.

Move closer to any potential "trouble spot". This is often enough to remind pupils to get back on task. When they even *start* to do the right thing, remember to Descriptively Praise every tiny step in the right direction.

Make yourself a focal point by using larger, more dramatic gestures than you ordinarily would. This will help you to capture the attention and interest of those pupils who are not "good at" listening and so might easily tune out your voice. An easy way to start gesturing more is to point frequently.

Smile a lot! Children respond positively to a pleasant, friendly facial expression, just as we do. We need to set a good example, especially on the days when we really don't feel like it! We usually remember to extend this simple courtesy to strangers, but often forget to do this in the rush and busyness of our classrooms. You may be concerned that it would be "artificial" or "insincere" to smile when you are annoyed, frustrated, etc. However, studies have shown that the physical act of smiling produces chemicals in the brain that actually make the person who is smiling (as well as the recipient of the smile) immediately feel friendlier, braver and more hopeful, even when there is absolutely *no* change in the external circumstances. So, do not wait until something pleases you in order to start smiling. Put yourself into a better frame of mind by smiling *before* there is any good reason to.

When you are having any interaction with a pupil (or even with a colleague!), however brief or seemingly unimportant, stop everything else that you are doing. Don't be marking exercise books, helping someone else at the same time, tidying up, etc. Pupils are learning something intangible from every interaction. They are either learning what we want them to learn (co-operation, self-reliance, compassion, tidiness, enthusiasm, pride in their work, etc.) or they are learning something else by default, often the very opposite! When we do not give pupils our full attention, they will learn that we are not taking them seriously or valuing them, and they will gradually lose respect for their teachers, for school and for learning.

When you are dealing with an individual pupil, the only other activity you can productively engage in is Descriptive Praise. The more pupils we Descriptively Praise, the better, because Descriptive Praise improves willingness and co-operation. Frequent sprinkles of Descriptive Praise can keep the rest of your class on task while you spend a few minutes with an individual pupil.

It becomes much easier to remember to stop everything and focus on only one pupil once we realise that every other pupil in the classroom is learning a valuable lesson from observing our concentration on that individual pupil. All the pupils are noticing that you are taking each pupil seriously and that you are willing to devote your full attention to being positive, firm and consistent. So, stop moving, establish eye contact and give the pupil your full attention.

Prepare for success by frequently Descriptively Praising pupils when they make eye contact. That will enable you to successfully require pupils to look at you when they are talking to you or listening to you. The easiest way to develop this habit is to stop talking as soon as a pupil looks away. When he looks back up, thank him and start again. Pupils will soon get the message.

Always face the pupils when speaking.

Keep your hands away from your face so that the pupils with auditory processing problems can watch your mouth.

Talk less and *do* more.

Chapter 4
Descriptive Praise

1. Different kinds of praise

It is a disconcerting fact that most of the praise and rewards we use when we are trying to motivate reluctant and resistant pupils have been proven to be largely ineffective.

Some pupils remain reluctant and resistant year after year, with very little improvement in their behaviour, attitudes or work habits. This is true even though teachers consistently report that it is the most problematic pupils who end up with the lion's share of the praise (as well as stars, stickers, special privileges and treats). Understandably, this state of affairs has been known to breed resentment amongst the pupils for whom co-operation and careful work are the norm.

"Evaluative praise" is the kind of praise that does not have much impact on behaviour or attitudes. It consists of well-worn phrases such as "You're so clever!", "What a beautiful drawing!", "Brilliant!", "Very good!", "Great job!", and of course the favourite, "Well done!".

Pupils who are frequently "in trouble" because of their misbehaviour or poor work habits simply do not believe this kind of praise, no matter how much of it they receive. This can be very discouraging for teachers, who may respond by redoubling their efforts to praise, with no visible results.

The good news is that there is a type of praise, called Descriptive Praise, that *has* been shown to motivate, to enhance self-esteem, to gently but firmly nudge pupils into more productive habits, and even to teach skills and information.

When we Descriptively Praise, we leave out the effusive, over-the-top phrases and simply say what we notice. Rather than pretending that something is wonderful or terrific when it isn't, we notice and mention all the tiny steps in the right direction, the actions that are just OK, and all the times when the pupil refrains from doing the wrong thing. This has been shown, in every instance where it is used consistently, to motivate children and teenagers to notice and change their own behaviour.

2. Using Descriptive Praise to improve all aspects of:

2a. Behaviour

1. Acting politely, considerately, positively (which includes the pupil's language and tone of voice)
2. Following instructions, including listening with the intention to comply
3. Following rules and routines
4. Staying on task
5. Paying attention to details

2b. Academic work

1. Accuracy
2. Thoroughness
3. Presentation
4. Creativity and problem-solving
5. Willingness, courage

2c. Social skills

1. Turn-taking, patience
2. Accepting others' views, opinions, choices, decisions, mannerisms, etc.
3. Respecting property
4. Being helpful, teamwork

In the first book, "In Step With Your Class", I gave 100 examples of Descriptive Praise, covering all of the above issues, so that teachers could see how it can be used to improve all aspects of behaviour, attitudes, work habits and peer relationships. In this book I am including even more examples in order to help teachers learn to feel comfortable with this new skill. Following are some more examples.

2a. Behaviour

A1. Following instructions

- You followed the instructions straight away.
- I see everyone is doing what I asked.
- The instructions are being followed by almost everyone in the room.
- You were able to repeat the instruction back to me when I asked you to, and you remembered most of it.
- Thank you for co-operating.
- You did it so quickly, with no wasting time.
- You did what I said, and you did it carefully.
- I asked people to listen politely, with no interrupting, and that's just what you're doing.
- It was brave of you all to follow my instructions, even though it felt scary for some of you to speak from the front of the classroom.

A2. Following rules and routines

- When I look at our bookcase, I see all the books standing up straight. That means people have been taking the time to follow the rule about putting them away carefully.
- Many of you have been keeping your desks clear of unnecessary items. You've been remembering our routine for tidying up at the end of each activity.
- All of you on this table remembered to bring everything we need for tracing. You remembered the routine.
- Thanks for following our morning routine so quickly and quietly.
- You remembered how I've told you to do it, and you did it that way. I didn't have to tell you.
- Every week we get ready for our art lesson in the same way. And this week I didn't have to remind anyone. You remembered the sequence, and you did it.

- Today, no one asked me how to do it. Most of you remembered the routine. And the people who didn't remember just looked around and saw what everyone else was doing. So you all did the right thing.
- I didn't have to prompt you to answer in a full sentence. You remembered that's what I expect from you.
- You don't agree with this rule, but you're following it anyway, without any arguing.
- You remembered to read that paragraph inside your head.

A3. Staying on task

- It looks like you're upset about what George said to you, but it hasn't stopped you from doing the right thing. You're still working. Even though you might feel like answering George, you're still working.
- Even though a lot of you are tired and hot and sweaty from double games, you're not complaining. You're focusing on your work.
- Everyone on this row is tracing and cutting out. No one is playing with the equipment.
- This topic might not seem very interesting, but when I look around the class I see most people quietly getting on with it.
- Even though you may not understand why you have to learn all about this, I see that you're still trying to answer my questions about it.
- It's the last lesson before lunch-time. I imagine you're starving and beginning to think about lunch. But no one's mentioned it. Most of you are carrying on labelling your diagrams.
- Just now when I went around the room and listened to each pair, I heard that most of you were on task. You were discussing your ideas for the project. You weren't talking about anything else.
- You're probably excited about the Christmas play this afternoon, and you might be feeling nervous, but you're not talking about it. You know it's time for Geography, so most of you are concentrating on your maps.

- The only sounds I can hear are people writing. Everyone is so quiet!

A4. Paying attention to details

- You're checking over your spelling. Instead of just saying you were finished, you're taking a few extra minutes to do your personal best.
- Maybe you didn't feel like rewriting that whole answer. But you wanted to include all the information, so you chose to rewrite it. You really want to be thorough.
- You noticed that James didn't come back after Music. Thank you for telling me. And you didn't shout it out; you remembered to put your hand up, and you waited until I called on you.
- Most of your sentences start with capital letters and end with full stops.
- You remembered to underline all the labels on your diagram.

A5. Acting politely, considerately and positively

- You're not just thinking about what you want. You're also thinking about what your team mates want.
- You're not touching anyone else's property. You're being respectful.
- You are not arguing; you're just accepting it.
- I haven't heard any of the teams arguing today.
- I appreciate that this class hasn't called anybody any names today, even when you got annoyed.
- I see pupils taking turns, not hogging the equipment.
- People are remembering to put hands up, instead of interrupting. That shows maturity and consideration.
- Even though you didn't like his idea, you were polite. You let him finish talking.
- You're coming up with lots of possible solutions!
- So many smiles!

- It's not easy to hand over the ball when you want to finish your game. But you did it without a fuss. You didn't say, "It's not fair".
- What a quiet table this is!

2b. Academic work

B1. Accuracy

- This whole side of the room followed my instructions exactly.
- Even though you don't like copying from the board, I can see that you took the time to do it neatly and carefully.
- No mistakes!
- This work will get lots of ticks because you remembered every single detail.
- Five of these answers are right.

B2. Thoroughness

- I see you have included everyone in your drawing of your family - even the cat!
- You worked on this for three lessons, until all the sea was blue and the earth was brown.
- This is the longest essay you have written this term.
- You included all the information a listener would need to be able to understand why the chemical reaction took place.

B3. Presentation

- You have made all your small letters the same height. They all come right up to the halfway line. That makes your writing look so neat.
- Your name, the date and your title are all in the correct place. It looks like you are really thinking about the right way to do things.
- Your shirt is tucked in, and your tie is the correct length. You look very mature.

B4. Willingness, courage

- You didn't give up, and you finally figured out how to solve that problem.
- I know you find this difficult but I can see you are trying. You have already written two lines.
- It doesn't come easily to you, but you are willing to have a go.
- You asked John about the next instruction. I see that you have been using your initiative instead of sitting around waiting.

2c. Social skills

C1. Turn-taking, patience

- You didn't push into the lunch queue even though I know you are starving!
- Thank you for being patient. You've had to wait a long time, and you haven't complained.
- You could see Tom was having problems, and you waited while I helped him. Thank you.

C2. Accepting others' views

- You're showing me that you are understanding that we can all have different opinions.
- Even though I could see you feel very strongly about this topic, you've been letting others speak.
- You took on board Ben's idea and used it after all, even though at first you thought it wouldn't work.

C3. Respecting property

- When you saw a hat on the ground, you could have walked right past it and left it there. Thanks for bringing it in.
- Your exercise book is still clean. Thanks for not drawing on it.
- You haven't been seen dropping litter in the lunchroom for two weeks now.
- I appreciate your telling me what you overheard about your classmates planning to spray-paint the playground wall. Your action shows respect for school property.

- Just now when you accidentally knocked Joseph's jacket off the hook, you stopped and put it back.

C4. Helpfulness, teamwork

- You could have gone ahead to get your lunch, but you stayed a bit longer to help us clean up – that's helpful. Now we can all go to lunch together.
- Going around the room just now, observing the different teams preparing for their presentations, I saw people encouraging the ones who were worried. I didn't see any teasing. You are really learning to support each other.
- Even though this team finished first, I haven't heard any bragging or boasting. If I were on one of those other teams, I'd really appreciate that!
- Even though this team finished last, I haven't heard any complaints or excuses. That's what's called "being a good sport". That way it's fun no matter who wins or loses.
- Thanks for opening the door so quickly because you could see my arms were full.

3. Points to remember about Descriptive Praise

3a. General points

- Use Descriptive Praise, rather than evaluative praise, so that the pupil knows exactly what he has done right, which makes it easier for him to do it again.
- Make a continuing effort to look for and find things to Descriptively Praise.
- Find specific actions to Descriptively Praise every day, especially actions that have required the pupil to make an effort, even if the result is still below average. This builds self-esteem much more than when we praise aspects of the pupil over which he has no control, such as being clever, pretty, or good at soccer.
- Descriptively Praise *every pupil every day* for behaviour or work habits that you want to see more of.

- One way to make sure you achieve this is to stand by the door at the beginning and end of each lesson and Descriptively Praise every pupil as he passes through the door.
- A daily checklist will let you know if your Descriptive Praise is reaching every pupil every day.

- Descriptive Praise of one pupil (or row or table) gives every pupil who hears it very useful information about what you expect. A ripple effect takes place.
- Descriptively Praising a table or group helps to build team spirit. Pupils feel more a part of the group, and they grow to like the group's members more.
- If you are frustrated by a pupil who keeps making "careless" mistakes, don't say: "If you would just pay attention!" Do say: "You've got 16 right out of 20, and I can see you understand how to add and subtract fractions. Now, it's time for corrections".
- When responding to a pupil's answer, question or comment, find something to agree with or to Descriptively Praise or to empathise with in everything the pupil says. This builds the pupils' confidence in himself, and helps the pupil feel valued.
- Remember that Descriptive Praise is the most powerful motivator there is.
- Descriptive Praise is the easiest, quickest and most effective way to keep a classroom running smoothly and to keep pupils co-operative, motivated and on task.

3b. Sentence starters

The easiest way to start your Descriptive Praise sentences is with the word "You". As you become comfortable with this skill you will want to inject some variety into the way you phrase your Descriptive Praise. Here is a short list of sentence-starters, in case you are not sure how to begin:

- I see that …
- I notice that …
- When I look around the classroom, I see that …

- When I look at this table/row/part of the room, I notice that …
- When I look at you, I see …
- What I can see is…
- Wherever I look, I see…
- I can hear…
- Robert and Alex are…
- This table is…
- I am pleased that …
- I am delighted that …
- It gives me great pleasure to see …
- Thank you for not …
- I am very impressed by …
- You did the right thing. You …

4. A frequently asked question

Question:

"I get so annoyed with the deliberate messing about of the most difficult pupils that I can't think of anything to praise, descriptively or otherwise. How can I find things to Descriptively Praise when faced with misbehaviour after misbehaviour?

My reply:

Most misbehaviour is minor rather than major and impulsive, compulsive or habitual rather than deliberate. It usually happens in short bursts. I suggest that you wait for a pause in the misbehaviour, then say something like:

"Thanks for stopping."

"You're not arguing any more."

"You didn't repeat that comment. Probably you realised that it was inappropriate."

"You started to bother your neighbour, but then you stopped. Now your hands are in the right place."

"No one's chatting on this table now. Everyone's silent."

Chapter 5
Reflective Listening

1. What is Reflective Listening?

Reflective Listening is a helpful tool that you can use whenever you sense that a pupil's uncomfortable emotions are getting in the way of focused, on-task behaviour. For some pupils that will be many times each day! Reflective Listening is a particular way of responding, in which we take the time and make the effort to try to understand what the pupil is feeling at that moment and then reflect back to him in words what we imagine he is feeling.

2. What are the benefits of Reflective Listening?

1. It helps the pupil to see that the teachers care about *him*, not just about his academic performance or whether he obeys the rules. Pupils who feel respected will become more respectful.
2. Reflective Listening helps the pupil to feel "heard" and understood. This is a reassuring feeling which can defuse uncomfortable emotions and potentially explosive situations. Many children and teens are confused and inarticulate about their feelings. They let the adults know that something is wrong not by talking about it but by acting up and misbehaving. Reflective Listening focuses on changing the pupil's mood, *not* on trying to change his mind.
3. It demonstrates that life is easier and more rewarding when we learn to recognise and manage our emotions. This skill has recently become known as "emotional literacy".
4. Over time, Reflective Listening teaches pupils a vocabulary for expressing their feelings in words, rather than acting out.

5. The experience of being heard and understood often enables the pupil to relax emotionally. He no longer "needs" to misbehave to make his point, so he automatically starts to put his attention towards problem-solving.

6. Used consistently, Reflective Listening almost always results in improved behaviour, social skills, motivation, co-operation and self-esteem.

For example, when a pupil is deliberately misbehaving or breaking a rule, it is tempting to automatically bark an order to stop. With the majority of pupils this will be enough to bring them to their senses, and they will stop misbehaving. But what about the very angry, resistant, possibly aggressive and intimidating pupil? A teacher's direct instruction may serve to fan the flames of further rebellion, especially if there is an audience of his peers and especially if the pupil already resents this teacher. To side-step potential explosions, I suggest that we make a rule for ourselves: only give a direct instruction if you are 95% sure that the pupil will comply. If you are *not* sure, you can Reflectively Listen instead. This may well soften, or deflect, the pupil's anger. It also enables the pupil to save face and the teacher to remain the authority.

3. When can we use Reflective Listening?

The pupils who experience the most distress at school are often the ones least able to express their feelings coherently. Instead of saying what is really troubling them, they may complain about insignificant things, accuse, insult and "tell on" their classmates, slouch and mutter and roll their eyes in disgust, and, of course ignore or refuse to co-operate with our rules, routines and instructions.

These pupils are expressing themselves in "code". We will need to become sensitive to their codes if we want to help them learn to manage their uncomfortable emotions safely and constructively.

It is all too easy to dismiss, ignore or minimise the endless stream of complaints and negative remarks:

- This is too hard.
- This is baby work.
- Miss, he's bothering me.
- My mum said I don't have to do this.
- I hate maths.
- I read this book last year.
- I never get to go first.
- This is so boring.
- I don't get it.
- I don't know what to do.
- Why do we have to?
- He's doing it too. Why don't you tell him off too?

In the same vein, we can easily drift into the habit of reacting with irritation to the myriad of annoying off-task behaviours that a few of our pupils keep on repeating no matter how many times they are told not to.

When we look below the surface of the minor and major misbehaviour, we find that these pupils are trying to cope with very painful feelings of frustration, failure, shame, vulnerability, anxiety, confusion, anger and even sometimes revenge.

4. How to Reflectively Listen

Reflective Listening has five steps, several of which are not so easy to do!

Step *ONE* consists of consciously and deliberately choosing to put our own emotions and wishes to one side temporarily. We may find ourselves feeling frustrated, irritated or even furious. Sometimes we might feel sorry for a pupil who is having a hard time. None of these emotions is helpful to our pupils. Strong feelings cloud our thinking and lead us to react, rather than to take the time to use each interaction wisely to teach and train. We can call ourselves back to order when we are tempted to react in ways that we know from experience do not move the pupil on towards greater self-awareness or self-control or self-confidence. At those times we can help ourselves to become more detached and more positive by vividly visualising scooping up our negative emotion (frustration, arrogance, despair, confusion, etc.) with both hands and placing it carefully at the side of the room, waiting for us if we want it back later. As silly as this strategy might sound, it has been proven to be very effective at helping people stay calm under very adverse circumstances.

In Step *TWO*, we stop whatever else we are doing and we listen. This is easier said than done in a busy classroom, when you are trying to keep five balls in the air, multi-tasking like mad.

To show that we are listening we can make what I call "telephone noises". During telephone conversations we often sprinkle our listening with sounds and phrases such as "Mm… Oh…Really?..." These utterances show the person on the other end of the telephone that we are still there, still listening, and still interested. Ordinarily we do not need so many of these noises in face-to-face conversations because the speaker can see from our facial expressions that we are listening and interested. But pupils with problems are notorious for misunderstanding or simply not noticing facial expressions. This weakness falls into the category of "dyssemia", a recently coined word that describes the difficulty that some people have understanding the meaning of symbols and representations. So let's make it easier for these pupils to register that we care and are listening.

In Step *THREE*, you imagine what the pupil is feeling *below* the level of his words. For example:
- "This is stupid" may mean "This work looks too hard".
- "Leave me alone" might mean "I am afraid I will lose my temper if you keep talking to me".
- "I hate this school" might be the only way the pupil knows how to express his feelings of failure and shame.
- "Everyone always picks on me." may be a safer way to express "What's wrong with me?".

It is all too easy to misread the "code" and assume that the complaining or misbehaving pupil is just doing it to wind you up. Remember that all behaviour is caused, and much misbehaviour is caused by pupils who do not know what else to do with the uncomfortable feelings of frustration, embarrassment or irritation.

This step requires us to ask ourselves: What feeling might drive the pupil to do this, say this, think this? We take an educated guess about what might be going on for him.

Step *FOUR* consists of reflecting back to the pupil what we imagine he is feeling, rather than trying to address his thoughts with logic or reassurance or a mini-lecture.

It may turn out that we guessed correctly, and the pupil might really appreciate being understood.

Or we may have guessed wrong. This is fine too. In Reflective Listening, it is our attempt to understand that is important. Sometimes the pupil will set us straight when we guess wrong, but sometimes he won't. Either way, the gradual benefits of Reflective Listening are still accruing.

Sometimes you will find that a pupil does not want to admit to feeling what he is feeling. This too is fine because the purpose of Reflective Listening is not to force a "confession" but to help pupils, *over time*, to feel comfortable with the wide range of their emotions and with words that describe emotions.

When pupils do unburden themselves, it is easy to respond with "I understand". But we can never really understand another person's experience, so pupils are justified in answering angrily, "No, you *don't* understand anything about me or my life!" So let's stick to Reflective Listening.

When Reflectively Listening to teenagers, we need to keep remembering how prickly and anxious they may feel. Many teenagers are easily embarrassed and may feel threatened, intimidated and patronised, even when we are doing our best to be kind, gentle and respectful. Teenagers may feel very exposed when we talk about feelings. We can often be more successful by being low-key and general when we reflect back. For example, instead of saying, "You might be feeling really disappointed that you didn't get chosen", you could say, "It looks like something's worrying you".

In Step *FIVE*, which is optional, you give the pupil his wishes in fantasy. This friendly, often humorous response often lightens the mood, at the same time showing that you care about him.

5. Sentence starters

Reflective Listening is not about trying to mind-read. Because we will never know what is going on in someone's mind, our Reflective Listening statements need to be tentative. We can say:

"Maybe you're feeling that…"
"Sometimes it feels…"
"It can be very annoying when…"
"You might be wishing…"
"You seem…"
"You look…"
"Probably you wish…"
"I can sense…"
"I guess…"
"I think…"
"I imagine…"
"It seems like…"
"This might be…"
"It can be…"

6. List of possible feelings

Here is a list of words that we can use in Step *FOUR*, when we are reflecting back to pupils how we imagine they might be feeling. Many of these words will be unfamiliar to your pupils; using these words in conjunction with their more familiar synonyms will gradually stretch your pupils' vocabulary.

accused
afraid
aggressive
alone
ambivalent
angry
annoyed
anxious
apologetic
apprehensive
ashamed
astonished
attacked
awful

belittled
betrayed
bitter
blamed
boxed in
bullied
burdened
burned out

cast off
cautious
challenged
cheated
cheerless
closed
competitive
compulsive
condemned
condemning
condescended to
confused

conspicuous
contrite
critical
criticised
crushed

dazed
defeated
defenceless
defensive
dejected
depressed
depressing
despairing
desperate
despised
despising
despondent
destructive
detestable
devalued
different
disappointed
discriminated against
disgusted
disorganised
displeased
dissatisfied
distracted
distressed
disturbed
dominated
doubted
doubting
dragged down
dreading

embarrassed
enraged
envious
exasperated
explosive
exposed

fearful
fed up
flustered
forgotten
fragile
frantic
frazzled
frightened
frustrated
furious

ganged up against
grumpy
guilty

hassled
hated
helpless
hopeless
humiliated
hurt

ignored
impatient
inadequate
incapable
inferior
infuriated
insecure
insulted
intimidated

intolerant
irate
irritable
irritated
isolated

jealous
judged
judgemental

left out
let down
lied about
lied to
lonely
lost
low

made fun of
manipulated
melancholy
messed about
miserable
misrepresented
mistreated
misunderstood
mixed emotions
mystified

negative
neglected
nervous
not listened to
not chosen
not sure what to do

obsessive
odd one out

outraged
over-loaded
over-looked
over-protected
over-protective
overwhelmed
over-worked

panicked
patronised
persecuted
pessimistic
picked on
powerless
precarious
pre-occupied
pressured
provoked
pushed
put down
put on the spot
puzzled

quarrelsome

rage
reckless
rejected
rejecting
reluctant
remorseful
resented
resentful
restless
ridiculed
rushed

sad
scared
sceptical
scorn
secretive
shaken
shame
shattered
shocked
shy
sick and tired
sorrowful
sorry
startled
stressed
stubborn
suffering
surprised
suspicious
swamped

tearful/teary
teased
tempted
tense
terrible
terrified
threatened
timid
tired out
told off
trapped
treated badly
treated unfairly
tricked
troubled

unable	unfulfilled	unwilling
unaccepted	unhappy	upset
unappreciated	unlovable	
uncertain	unloved	victimised
unconfident	unloving	vulnerable
unco-operative	unnoticed	wary
undecided	unprepared	weepy
underestimated	unsatisfied	withdrawn
undermined	unsettled	worn down
uneasy	unsuccessful	worn-out
unforgiven	unsure	worried
unforgiving	unwanted	
		yearning

7. Examples of Reflective Listening

Here are some typical phrases that have been used successfully by teachers with pupils:

7a. You're probably angry about all this writing you have to do. I know you really hate writing.

"Hate" and "angry" are strong words. Teachers may be wary of using such intense language in case the words somehow influence the pupil to feel even more upset than he already is. The reality is that for the sub-section of the class exhibiting habitual non-co-operation (whether avoidance, negative attention-seeking or defiance) these strong words are an accurate reflection of how they feel. They really do *hate* having to do the things they are not good at:

- sitting still
- listening for any length of time
- keeping their thoughts in their head
- putting their hands up before speaking
- persevering with a task that seems completely irrelevant to their day-to-day concerns

- paying attention to details
- and, of course, writing.

Feeling understood often helps pupils to relax a bit and approach an uncomfortable task more positively.

7b. I imagine that right now you're feeling ignored and left out because I was listening to someone else first. Maybe it seems as if I don't care about how you feel.

This Reflective Listening sentence describes the inner landscape of many of the pupils who habitually argue, whinge, talk too loudly or interrupt.

7c. Maybe you're wishing you never had to do spelling ever again.

Spelling is a blight on the existence of many pupils with problems. When we voice what they are probably feeling, they feel less criticised and judged. You need not worry that your Reflective Listening will mislead pupils into thinking that they never have to do spelling again. The word "wish" clearly differentiates between fact and fantasy. A pupil might react to this Reflective Listening statement with "Yeah, why do we have to? It's stupid (or boring)!" If you get the sense that the pupil is still just complaining, keep Reflective Listening. However, if it seems that the pupil really wants to know why he has to do spelling (or any other task), do not start explaining or justifying. Instead, ask him to take a sensible guess, and then find something to Descriptively Praise in his response, if only the fact that he was willing to think about it instead of saying "I don't know".

7d. It can be so frustrating when someone else gets there first.

Extreme and unreasonable competitiveness is a frequent feature of pupils with poor social skills and low self-esteem. This can manifest as boasting or always trying to be best or first or get the most. Sometimes a highly competitive pupil may react in the opposite manner, withdrawing, not even trying, assuming that he can never do as well as the others. Once again, bringing this feeling of intense competitiveness into the open through Reflective Listening helps the pupil to begin to understand himself, gives him words for his feelings, and shows that we understand and are not blaming or judging.

7e. Being called names by a friend can be very confusing. You thought he liked you, but now you're wondering if you can trust him.

Pupils with a lot of anger and very little self-control often are described as having "immature social skills". Sometimes they are bullied; sometimes they are the bullies; often they switch from one role to the other in different parts of their life. Time and again, their accusatory stance alienates their peers. Helping pupils to explore their own reactions is far more effective at changing ingrained patterns of reacting than having the perpetrator go through the motions of an often insincere apology.

7f. It's hard to settle down to work when you're worried that you might make a mistake.

Underneath the swearing, door-slamming, shoving and arguing back, these pupils are often very anxious. The more we can articulate this for them, the sooner they will be able to communicate in words, rather than by misbehaviour.

Anxiety is a large part of why some pupils regularly resist tackling the learning tasks that we set them. It is easy for teachers to misread the signals and assume that the habit of time-wasting is caused by factors that teachers cannot influence. Luckily, teachers can do a lot to improve the academic competence and confidence of our pupils. We can modify the way we present lessons to make them more "inclusion-friendly"; you will find many ideas for doing that in this book and in the companion volume, 'In Step With Your Class'. We can also commit ourselves 100% to *never* giving a pupil work to do that we suspect may be too difficult for him to be successful with. Otherwise we are guilty of unintentionally tormenting, rather than educating, our pupils.

7g. You might be feeling anxious about how to tackle this project. Big projects can be daunting.

Projects are a nightmare for pupils who have problems with attention, organisation, planning, sequencing and time-management. In addition to Reflective Listening, we also need to make the tasks *completely manageable* for them. Otherwise they will learn nothing from the project except that they are no good at doing projects. To make projects useful as training tools that help pupils establish good habits, we need to have pupils practise breaking down an indigestible whole into bite-sized chunks:

1. Differentiate by having simpler projects with fewer sections.
2. Make all rules absolutely clear. Make all implicit expectations explicit.
3. Assign sections to be done on different days, rather than the whole project to be due on one date.
4. Check each section, giving feedback.
5. Require pupils to expand or rewrite, paying attention to all details.
6. Celebrate completion – it is a huge achievement!

7h. I can see from your face (or by the way you are sitting, or by the fact that you're not working, etc.) that something is bothering you.

This is a useful Reflective Listening sentence for the many times when you are faced with a pupil who is grumpy or withdrawn or argumentative and you have no idea what he is feeling.

8. A frequently asked question

Question:

"This all seems like an unnecessarily long, drawn-out process. When we see that a pupil is upset, why can't we just ask him "What's the matter?""

My reply:

>Occasionally you will come across a pupil who knows how he feels and can put it into words clearly and wants to share his feelings with you. By all means, ask this pupil "What's the matter?"

>However, most children and young people, even those without any learning difficulties, have a hard time knowing what they are upset about. A typical immature response is to blame someone else. When we ask "What's the matter?" or "What happened?" we get a blow-by-blow account of what the other person did wrong. No useful learning comes from that.

>It is easy to forget that our pupils are always communicating with us through their behaviour. Misbehaviour is often a sign that a pupil is experiencing an uncomfortable emotion or is desperately trying to avoid experiencing an uncomfortable emotion. It may be hard to believe that the simple act of reflecting back to a pupil what we imagine he is feeling can improve attitudes and behaviour. Try it consistently for two to four weeks and see what happens.

Chapter 6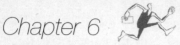
Giving instructions

This chapter is all about how we can modify our verbal and non-verbal language to maximise the likelihood that our pupils will follow our instructions. This is extremely important because if our pupils do what we tell them to do, then most behaviour problems are eliminated. You may be sceptical: "Surely it's not that simple! Isn't there a whole lot more to gaining co-operation and improving motivation than just knowing how to get pupils to follow instructions?".

Of course there is. If you think about it, though, you will realise that following instructions is, indeed, the basis of co-operation, as well as being the first step towards self-reliance and self-motivation, both of which are our eventual goals for our pupils. This view may seem overly simplistic. After all, we have been taught that teaching is a highly complex art or science. I am not denying this. What I am saying is that effective teaching and effective learning can only take place when the pupil is ready, willing and able to learn, in other words, when the pupil is *co-operating* with the learning process.

So in the following pages I will give you specific step-by-step suggestions for:

- What to do before giving instructions
- What to do when giving instructions
- What to do after giving instructions (following through).

1a. What to do before giving instructions

1a. Stop everything else you are doing and look at the pupil

Do not tell the pupil to do something (or to stop doing something) until you have made the time in your day to pursue the matter thoroughly. This is important because every time we do *not* follow through, we are "training" our pupils to take us less and less seriously.

When you have something to say to your pupil, stop everything. Give your pupil your full attention; do not be doing anything else.

Make (and maintain) eye contact before, during and after giving instructions or stating expectations to your pupil. You cannot do this if you are writing on the whiteboard, looking at someone's work or answering a question.

1b. Have the pupil stop everything he is doing and look at you

When you are about to give instructions or state expectations, make sure that your pupils stop everything *before you even begin to speak*. This means they must not be looking at a book, fiddling with a pen, chatting to a friend, doodling, interrupting, etc. They need to be looking and listening and doing nothing else.

To get the attention of the whole class and to help put them in a co-operative mood:
- stand up straight, doing nothing else besides waiting
- in a loud voice, Descriptively Praise and smile at *any* pupil who:
  - is in his seat
  - is quiet
  - is looking at you
  - has the right equipment ready
  - is not playing with something
  - is facing the front
  - is sitting up straight
  - etc.

Waiting combined with Descriptive Praise works better than simply telling the class or individual pupils to be quiet or to pay attention because:

- The atmosphere stays calmer and more pleasant.
- Attention is going to the positive behaviour. As pupils gradually notice other pupils getting Descriptive Praise for correct behaviour, a ripple effect spreads through the group. More and more pupils start paying attention.
- All children and teenagers naturally desire the approval of adults who show they care. Even disruptive children and teenagers will start to see that they can earn the teacher's approval easily and *quickly*, simply by sitting still, facing forward, looking at the teacher, etc.

If, while you are talking, a pupil's gaze shifts from your face, stop talking instantly and wait with a smile on your face until he looks at you again. When he does look at you again, smile, thank him, and start talking again.

Do not give a pupil any instruction or state an expectation until you have helped him to feel *relatively* friendly and willing. Reflective Listening is very useful for this. If you skip this step you are likely, with certain pupils, to get a negative response. We want to reduce the number of these negative responses (whether they manifest as avoidance, attention-seeking or defiance) so that willingness and co-operation begins to feel easy, natural, even pleasurable.

2. What to do when giving instructions

2a. Tell the pupil what to do simply, clearly, and only once

Since you are only going to be giving the instructions once, you can see how important it is for you to get your pupils' full attention first.

Smile when giving instructions.

Talk slowly and clearly. (See Chapter 3 for a discussion of how to use language consciously and constructively.) Keep pausing after each part of the instruction to let your words sink in. This is especially important with pupils who have auditory processing weaknesses.

Keep impatience, frustration, and anger out of your voice. An annoyed or frustrated tone in your voice understandably makes pupils stop listening because it is so unpleasant.

Use humour, Descriptive Praise and Reflective Listening to keep the tone friendly, but stay focused, calm and *determined*.

Do not use too many words.

Use definite statements when talking with your pupil. If you are not giving the pupil a choice in the matter, do not ask questions or make statements that seem to imply that they have a choice or that you are merely suggesting or requesting:
- "Would you like to...?"
- "How about...?"
- "Don't you think you should...?"
- "I really think you should..."

Also, do not tack "OK?" on to the end of a sentence if you are not giving the pupil a choice about something. These indefinite ways of talking are confusing and misleading, especially for pupils with language problems.

Do not repeat yourself! Repeating often unwittingly trains the pupil not to listen properly or not to feel he has to respond the first time (or even the first three times!).

Be very, very clear and very, very specific in ALL of your instructions and expectations.

Do not ever tell a pupil to do something unless you are willing to:
- stick to your decision
- check up to find out whether your instructions were carried out correctly and thoroughly
- follow through by giving consequences for compliance or non-compliance.

You could be worried that a pupil would simply refuse to comply and you might be left not knowing how to make him follow your instructions. It is true that we *cannot make* our pupils do anything, but we *can influence* them to be more willing and less resistant. Only give instructions after you have prepared for success and influenced the pupil so that he is *very likely* to comply. All the strategies in this book will help your pupils become more and more willing.

Think carefully before you require something, so that you are not tempted to negotiate. You may think that your willingness to negotiate is a sign of flexibility, but the pupil is probably learning that if he argues you will eventually change your mind.

To teach responsibility, do not give a pupil the privilege of making choices until he has earned it through sensible behaviour.

When you do offer choices make sure that:
- The choices are appropriate to the level of his developmental needs, rather than to his wants.
- The choices are within the limits of what you feel is right or what you feel must be done. Whenever you offer your pupils choices, you need to feel *totally* comfortable with whichever of the options the pupils might choose.
- Most of the time, limit the choices to only two. This reduces confusion and time-wasting. Occasionally a particular task will call for a wider range of options.
- Warn pupils in advance that they have only a limited time period (maybe one minute) in which to decide on their choice. After the time limit is up, if they have not chosen, you will choose for them.
- Also warn pupils in advance that they need to consider very carefully because once they have chosen, they are not allowed to change their minds. This may seem cruel, but it is a good lesson in how real life often works. If pupils are allowed to change their mind after choosing, they are not learning to slow down and think ahead. When pupils are not held accountable in this way, their first "choice" is really not much more than an impulsive blurt.

Do not say: "You have to do a book report on this particular book". (No choice)

Do not say: "What book would you like to choose for your book report?". (Too much choice)

Do say: "For your book report, you can choose any one of the ten books on this list". (Say this after you have selected books that are appropriate in terms of comprehension level, suitable language, values and literary merit.)

Do not justify or apologise for your rules, your standards, or your insistence on compliance. Apologising implies that we think we are in the wrong. If you really think the rules and standards are wrong, then work to change them or change your job! Of course, if you really have done something wrong, apologising sets a good example and shows pupils that you care about them. However, if you find yourself having to apologise more than once or twice a term, it probably means that you are over-reacting because you are stressed and frazzled from using ineffective strategies. Practising the techniques in this book will help you get back in charge of your emotions and of your class.

2b. Have the pupils say in their own words what they have to do and why

To make sure everyone knows what to do and how to do it, have pupils do a brief "pair-share", in which pupils explain to each other exactly what they think the instructions require them to do. The "pair-share" is complete only when both members of the pair have *exactly* the same understanding of what is required.

Have the pupils repeat *all the details* of your instructions back to you. One reason for doing this is to make sure that they understand exactly what is expected of them. This is a good way to check whether the task is too difficult or your language is too complicated or too quick. Also, children and teenagers are more likely to feel morally obligated to do what *they say* they will do, whereas they may well tune out, dismiss or ignore instructions if they do not have to respond with anything more than a nod of the head or a grunt.

Make sure that your pupils know *why* you want what you want. But instead of explaining, *ask them to tell you* why this instruction or policy is necessary or important.

Remember that when pupils respond to an instruction with "Why?" or "Do I have to?" or "Why do I have to?", this is rarely a genuine request for information, so do not repeat yourself or launch into an explanation. Your pupils have heard it all before, and they can, and should, work out for themselves the reason for the instruction. In fact, they probably *do* know the reason. "Why?" is often a diversionary ploy, a habit that may unconsciously serve to sidetrack the discussion, wind up the teacher, put off complying, find a loophole, waste time, confuse the teacher, weaken the teacher's resolve, etc.

2c. When the pupil does not understand the instructions

When a pupil shows by his actions or facial expression (or lack of expression!), or by his questions, that he has not understood you, do not simply repeat yourself! When we repeat instructions, we unwittingly "train" our pupils not to pay attention the first time. Instead of repeating or reminding, find out where the problem lies. An effective way to do this is by using Reflective Listening, discussed in Chapter 5. Chapter 3 has a section, "Answering pupils' questions", which talks about how to help pupils who are stuck or confused.

Once you have an idea what the pupil is confused about, require him to stretch himself to remember or try to figure it out by asking him to "Take a guess." Then WAIT. Do not accept "I don't remember" or "I don't know".

When you have asked a pupil to take a guess and he just sits there in silence, Descriptively Praise tiny steps in the right direction. For example, you could say, in all honesty:
- "Even though you don't know the answer, you haven't given up. You're not saying you don't know."
  Or
- "Even though you're not sure what to do next, you've written your name and you're still holding your pencil."

Consistently applied, this policy of not repeating yourself will soon be saving you time and aggravation at the same time as it builds self-reliance in your pupils.

In case you are worrying that this process might take forever in your classroom, the truth is that sometimes it does take more time at first. On the other hand, think of all the time currently spent on repeating and reminding. Determination and patience are necessary when we commit ourselves to training pupils to use their common sense. But it is an investment that will start to pay off in time saved within a few weeks.

When required to guess about the meaning of an instruction or expectation, pupils will usually dredge up an answer from their memory, or they will take a sensible guess. Either way, what they come up with is generally completely correct or nearly correct or correct but incomplete. This shows us that their confusion is rarely total. Often, the pupil *has* understood what to do and how to do it but is not confident that he understands. When this state of affairs is chronic, we call it "learned helplessness".

After the pupil has taken a guess, you may well find that you need to re-explain something. Again, asking questions of our pupils is often the best way to get them to think, rather than spoon-feeding them the answers.

2d. When the pupil has a complaint about the instructions

Even when you prepare for success by following all the advice in this book, at first you may continue to get a negative reaction, such as a grimace, rolling of the eyes, muttering, arguing, pleading, ignoring or outright refusal. In the first few weeks of putting these ideas into practice, be ready to spend lots of time Reflectively Listening, i.e. listening to the feelings behind his words (see Chapter 5). Be willing to understand and accept the pupil's feelings about the instructions or expectations and the accompanying consequences. This is not the same thing as agreeing with him. Reflective Listening and acceptance can defuse negative feelings, *yours as well as the pupil's,* and can show the pupil that you are "on his side".

I am assuming that you usually think carefully before you speak, and that therefore your instructions are well thought out, necessary, and worthy of being complied with. Do not let the strength of the pupil's upset feelings or resistance tempt you to change your mind or modify your instructions. Every time we modify our requirements we weaken our credibility and authority. Unintentionally we give reluctant and resistant pupils permission to argue with us or ignore us. And we give them an unrealistically rosy picture of real life, particularly the world of work.

3. What to do after giving instructions (following through)

3a. Stand and wait for compliance

After giving a *very short* set of instructions, wait for the actions to be carried out before giving the next very short set of instructions.

I am suggesting that you *stand* while you wait because standing signifies intention, authority, definiteness and determination. It is almost impossible for a pupil to disregard a teacher who is standing next to him. Although he may try to pretend that he does not see you, within a minute or so he will look up. When he sees your smile and hears your Descriptive Praise or Reflective Listening, his natural desire to please the people who care about him will urge him, gradually, to co-operate.

You may be thinking, at this point, that there are a lot of times and situations when teachers simply cannot stand and wait for very long. Of course, this is true. That is why I emphasise laying the foundations; by that I mean teaching and training the important attitudes and habits which, over time, will increase your pupils' motivation and willingness to co-operate so that you will *rarely* find yourself needing to wait more than a few seconds.

Be firm and consistent in your expectations and rules; do not waver.

When a pupil does not comply with an instruction, start with the assumption that there is an element of confusion, inattentiveness, impulsivity or of delayed auditory processing, even if you are almost certain that avoidance, attention-seeking or defiance are also involved.

When pupils do not immediately co-operate, we need to resist the natural human urge to: repeat, cajole, explain, entreat, preach, justify, etc. In a misguided attempt to save time, we may find ourselves trying to convince pupils that they should *want* to co-operate. Instead, we need to always be focusing on how we can create an amosphere in the classroom that generates co-operation and willingness. For example, Descriptively Praise anything you can find that is good, or OK, or even partially OK. This results in more co-operation and keeps the atmosphere friendlier and more positive. I know that Descriptive Praise may be the last thing you feel like doing when faced with a mini-insurrection. It seems counter-intuitive to Descriptively Praise when pupils are *not* complying, but it works! As I said before, Descriptive Praise is the most powerful motivator and training tool I have ever come across.

Stay with a resistant pupil while he begins to follow the instruction, until you are absolutely sure that he will carry it out properly, through to completion, without you.

3b. While you are standing and waiting, Descriptively Praise and Reflectively Listen to every small step in the right direction

After telling pupils to do (or to stop doing) something, a busy teacher might find that it is all too easy to shift focus to the next task and therefore:

- not even notice if all the pupils have done as you ask, or
- notice the compliance or lack of compliance but be too pre-occupied to address it.

This is understandable but counter-productive. To get more of the behaviour or academic performance that we want, we need to notice and mention every tiny step towards it.

Be patient with even the slowest progress. Becoming impatient will not motivate the resistant pupils to co-operate. Chronically non-co-operative pupils have had a great deal of annoyance directed towards them. In self-defence, they long ago perfected the art of letting all that impatience, annoyance and irritation wash right over them. Even threats, shouting and punishments hardly seem to get their attention.

Be willing to appreciate the pupil's effort, even when the result is not yet satisfactory, or is only partially satisfactory. This gives pupils permission to be learners (to be human!) and to make mistakes. Do not lecture them about "Everyone makes mistakes. You can't learn anything without making mistakes", etc. Our reaction when a pupil makes a mistake can help him to feel safe and accepted or can add to his embarrassment and anxiety.

When Descriptively Praising, stop everything else so that you can give the pupil your full attention. Look him in the eye and tell him something specific that you are pleased about. Explain why it pleases you.

Focus your Descriptive Praise on the details of how the pupils complied (quickly, politely, quietly, carefully, without grabbing, etc.). This reinforces what we mean by co-operation far better than the standard mini-lectures after something has gone wrong. See Chapter 4 for examples of Descriptive Praise.

Descriptively Praise even the smallest steps towards compliance, even when done with bad grace. Reflective Listening is a useful strategy for addressing the complaining, arguing, desklid-slamming, etc. With Reflective Listening, you are showing that you care about the pupil's feelings, and you are also showing that you are not getting wound up by the accompanying misbehaviour.

Combining Descriptive Praise and Reflective Listening is often very effective: "It can be frustrating having to look words up in the dictionary. I can see that you are getting impatient, but the dictionary is still open in front of you. You haven't given up." Or, "You're having a good time out here. It looks like you don't want to come in from break now, but you are facing in the right direction for coming in."

What about when there are *no* small steps in the right direction to Descriptively Praise?

1. As soon as you are aware that a pupil is not following your instructions (and this should be almost instantly because co-operation is the priority, definitely taking precedence over subject matter), stop everything! You need to show that you can see what he is doing (or not doing).

2. Trust your instincts when you sense that the pupil is testing your limits and your firmness; he may be doing just that! Remember, you are the adult, the teacher, the one in charge. Keep calm, but *do not ignore* the behaviour. Ignoring will often cause an escalation of the problem behaviour because the pupil is often looking for attention, and will continue to do whatever he is in the habit of doing to get attention.

3. Simply moving physically closer to the problem is usually effective: by the time you arrive at the hot spot, often the pupil has, albeit with bad grace, begun to comply. At that point you Descriptively Praise.

4. Sometimes nothing more than stopping in mid-sentence and giving a quizzical (not annoyed) look is needed. This conveys your surprise that the pupil is not doing what he should and also your calm confidence that he soon will.

5. You may need to say, "Hold on here" or "Wait" and then give your look. "Hold on here" is more likely to engage the pupil's willingness than "Stop!" or "Don't do that!" or "Why aren't you paying attention?"

6. You can ask him or another pupil, "What did I just say?" or "What should you be doing now?" When he repeats the instruction himself or hears it from another pupil (rather than from the teacher, whom he may resent on principle), this is often enough to prompt action. Then Descriptively Praise of course.

7. In the book, "In Step With Your Class", I discuss in detail how to be the "captain" of your classroom, how to use organisation, routines and follow-through to increase motivation and co-operation and to reduce avoidance, negative attention-seeking and defiance.

Chapter 7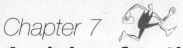
A vision for the future

What can teachers achieve by following the suggestions in this book? Based on all the reports from teachers who have persevered with these techniques, I predict that:

- You will be able to give more of your time to truly personalised teaching because you will be spending less time on "crowd control". Your classes will be calmer, easier and happier.
- You will learn more about what works and what does not work to bring out the best in even your most difficult pupils.
- Pupils with specific learning difficulties will improve their academic skills, behaviour, attention and social skills.
- You will establish a positive, firm and consistent atmosphere that will benefit you and your pupils.
- Your pupils will be more eager to learn and more willing to behave considerately.
- You will have the satisfaction of knowing that you are accomplishing your goals.
- You will be able to connect again with the ideals that first brought you into teaching.
- You will feel re-energised, re-inspired and re-empowered. You will get unstuck and get back in charge, which can prevent or even reverse 'burn-out'.
- You will have the time, patience and confidence to try out even more new techniques (from other sources) for improving the lives of pupils with special educational needs.

Does this sound too good to be true? I suggest that you keep an open mind and practise these new techniques, plus those in the companion volume, for two to four weeks and see what happens.

After all, what have you got to lose?

About the author

Noël Janis-Norton, founder and director of The New Learning Centre in London, is a learning and behaviour specialist with over 30 years' experience in England and the United States as a teacher, special needs advisor, consultant, lecturer, head teacher and parenting facilitator.

Noël is a mother of two, a foster parent and a grandmother who is passionate about empowering children and adults to fulfil their potential. To achieve this she uses, and teaches parents and professionals to use, her highly effective and thoroughly tested "Calmer, Easier, Happier" parenting and teaching methods.

As well as consulting with schools and leading workshops across the UK and in the US, Noël Janis-Norton is still very much a hands-on practitioner. She continues to teach, to work with families and to train professionals.

"Calmer, Easier, Happier Teaching and Learning" workshops

Turning theory into practice: In-service training for teachers, learning support assistants, learning mentors and SENCOs in nurseries, primary and secondary schools and special units.

Addressing the needs of pupils who have:
- atypical learning styles and/or
- problems with behaviour, confidence or motivation, whether they have a diagnosed difficulty or not.

These courses are interactive and contain many useful examples. The skills taught are practical and pro-active. Using the skills makes classroom management easier, and helps all pupils to achieve their best. By putting the new skills into practice, teachers can help pupils to be more:
- motivated and able to stay on task for longer
- confident and self-reliant

- polite, considerate and self-aware
- willing to follow rules, routines and instructions
- creative at problem-solving
- successful academically.

Popular in-service topics for schools are:
- Improving classroom behaviour
- Helping the atypical learner to thrive, not just survive
- Preventing and reducing bullying
- Involving parents as partners in education
- Raising standards through effective differentiation
- Harnessing the learning strengths of pupils with learning difficulties
- Reducing teacher stress and burn-out

Half-days, full days, weekends, evenings or twilight sessions

"The most interesting course I've been on for some time – constructive, informative, motivating."

"Noel's ideas work! As I keep practising the skills, I find that I like my pupils more and more."

"This course changed how I relate to my pupils. I now teach my pupils *how* to do their best."

"I just wish I had known about all these skills when I first started teaching."

"Stimulating material, presented with clarity and conviction. Thanks!"

"Very interesting content, well delivered. Modelling realistic scenarios."

The New Learning Centre also runs parenting skills classes for parents within schools, helping parents to improve their children's co-operation, motivation, confidence and schoolwork.

Back On Track

For more than 18 years, Noël and her team of skilled, highly experienced teachers and trainers have helped many families whose children are experiencing problems, ranging from mild to severe.

Back On Track is an intensive, short-term programme which helps children and teenagers who are struggling with emotional, behavioural or learning difficulties at school or at home.

When parents answer "Yes" to any of the following questions, we design a tailor-made programme for the family which can include seminars, ongoing classes, Family Learning Sessions and Parent Sessions, both in person and by telephone:

- Is your child experiencing difficulties at school?
- Does he find schoolwork or homework difficult, or making friends a challenge?
- Are you worried that he might be suspended or excluded?
- Is your child not attending school at all, due to exclusion or refusal?

Topics addressed include:

- Effective homework strategies
- Maximising co-operation
- Enhancing motivation and self-reliance
- Helping children and teens to express their feelings constructively
- Reducing sibling squabbles
- Parents learning to become a United Front
- Preparing children for change.

In our Family Learning Sessions, we work with the whole family, teaching the child and *at the same time* showing the parents how to help improve the child's academic and social skills, his confidence, motivation, self-esteem and anger-management.

If you would like to know more about the "Calmer, Easier, Happier" parenting and teaching methods, please contact in the U.K.:

Address: The New Learning Centre,
              211 Sumatra Road, London, NW6 1PF
Telephone: 020 7794 0321
E-mail: admin@tnlc.info
Website: www.tnlc.info

and in the U.S.A.:

Address:	"Calmer, Easier, Happier"
	Jessica Tevis, Bay Area Co-ordinator
	P.O. Box 574, Novato, CA, 94948-0574
Telephone:	415 419 3518
E-mail:	jbtdesign@mindspring.com
Website:	www.tnlc.info

"Calmer, Easier, Happier Parenting" Audio Tapes, CDs and Books

> How To Be A Better Parent
> By Cassandra Jardine
>
> The book is based on Cassandra's experience with The New Learning Centre and contains plenty of practical tips, written in an engaging style!

Audio Tapes and CDs

1 Descriptive Praise: The Greatest Motivator

A talk with Noël Janis-Norton. Learn what Descriptive Praise is and listen to a group of parents sharing their successful experiences of using Descriptive Praise.

2 Positive Discipline: What To Do When Your Child Says No

A talk with Noël Janis-Norton. Listen to a group of parents discussing how to establish routines which decrease parent-child conflicts and enable children to learn the vital skills of self-discipline.

3 Getting Back in Charge: The 6 Step Method

A talk with Noël Janis-Norton. Learn how to use the 6 Step Method to achieve co-operation, and listen to a group of parents sharing their experiences of using this highly effective procedure.

4 Descriptive Praise For Beginners

Noël Janis-Norton explains why Descriptive Praise is so powerful and gives over 100 examples of actual phrases you can use with your children. (Companion to tape 1)

5 The Challenge Of Being A Lone Parent

A talk with Noël Janis-Norton. Listen to a group of parents sharing experiences of the challenges faced by lone parents. Learn how the "Calmer, Easier, Happier" parenting skills can be used to greatly improve family life. This tape is extremely useful for two-parent families as well, especially if one parent is often away from home.

6 Unavailable at present

7 Boys Becoming Men: Changes, Choices & Challenges

A talk with Noël Janis-Norton. Listen to a group of parents discussing the challenges facing boys and young men and what mothers and fathers can do to help boys become their best selves.

8 Reflective Listening: Understanding Your Child

A talk with Noël Janis-Norton and a group of parents. Learn why and how Reflective Listening can help children and teenagers to understand themselves better and to express their feelings more constructively.

Prices:

Tapes @ £7 each + £0.50 p&p
CDs @ £9 each + £0.50 p&p
How To Be a Better Parent @ £11 + £2.00 p&p
In Step With Your Class @ £12.99 + £2.00 p&p

If you enjoyed this book why not read …

In Step with your Class
By Noël Janis-Norton
In the companion volume to *Learning to Listen, Listening to Learn*, Noël Janis-Norton shows how to maximize the strengths and minimize the problems of an atypical learner. The book addresses motivation, confidence, behaviour and basic skills.

- Practical advice to make classroom management easier and help pupils achieve their best.
- Written by a specialist with a wealth of experience working with children, teachers and parents.

ISBN 1-84299-217-1

Walk in their Shoes
By Edwina Cole
Fitting in with a school community can be a complex and often daunting experience, especially if you see the world in a slightly different way. Following extensive interviews, this book examines the experience of a typical school day for students with dyslexia, dyspraxia, ADHD, Asperger syndrome and speech and language difficulties.

- Helps you understand what goes through the minds of pupils with specific learning difficulties.
- A 'must read' for everyone involved in making education a positive experience.
- Written by an expert practitioner.

ISBN 1-84299-162-0

You can order these books direct from:

Macmillan Distribution Ltd, Brunel Road, Houndmills, Basingstoke, Hampshire RG21 6XS

Tel 01256 302699

Email: mdl@macmillan.co.uk